A WAR IN THE DISTANCE

HATJE
CANTZ

UKRAINE AND THE RETURN OF HISTORY

EDITED BY
EKATERINA DEGOT
AND
DAVID RIFF

Contents

In her essay for this volume, writer Maja Haderlap poignantly describes the feeling of living through a portentous moment whose importance we have yet to recognize fully. As she writes, the war in Ukraine, still distant, marks a major historical tipping point. But strangely, life continues in pursuit of happiness and creature comforts, overshadowed by the schema of militarization. Adding to the carbon footprint and the energy demands of our societies, such efforts at self-assurance only make matters worse, essentially feeding what she calls "fossil empires," their toxic leaders, and, like now in Ukraine, their genocidal military campaigns. Russia's war of aggression is a wake-up call. It is time to take responsibility for our daily activities, writes Haderlap. Our awareness of their impact is unprecedented, but so is the sense of paralysis and overwhelmingness that they bring.

During the preparations for the 2022 edition of steirischer herbst, there was no way to ignore the full-fledged invasion and occupation of Ukraine by the Russian Federation, or the deep seismic waves it has spread beyond the region and throughout the world. Its impact will be epoch-making and global. Yet the contours of the changes to come are yet unknown. Will Ukraine fend off these attempts at imperialist revanche and thus defend the rest of the world from its spreading? Or will the virus of a new fascism infect our incorrigible societies?

Precisely that uncertainty makes it so tempting to continue "as normal," to contain combat to a limited area of operations and to pretend that nothing has changed. Meanwhile, Putinism is not just a problem in the Russian Federation. Vladimir Putin's brand of politics until recently had a huge international fan club, providing the paradigm for new authoritarian populisms, some of which received the Kremlin's direct material support. All over the world, half-forgotten dreams of national palingenesis and imperial revanchism reappeared

as if out of nowhere, and with them the really
existing histories of Europe's crumbling empires,
its rejuvenated nations, and its fascist history,
fastidiously hidden in plain sight.

It was this complex and growing altered
perception of the present and dredging-up of
the irrepressible past that became one of the
central topics of the festival edition *A War in the
Distance*, which looked more broadly at what the
war might mean in a postfascist, postimperial,
neoliberal Europe, while continuously highlighting
the connection to current events. The present
reader reflects this approach. With its combination
of essays and shorter literary texts, it looks at
the narrower and broader impact of the war in
Ukraine, the histories it activates, and the futures it
might decide from different angles, some of them
quite far away, others up close.

Even from afar, the war is a constant media
presence, perhaps uniquely so. Telegram
channels and Twitter feeds have been providing
minute-by-minute coverage, countering claims of
fake news with verifiably gory footage and facts.
Images are uniquely implicated in the war and
bring it right into your pocket and onto your mobile
device—the same kind of device that can be used as
a weapon of war. Media theorist Olexii Kuchanskyi's
contribution explores the specificity and agency of
such images. His essay departs from a characteristic
battlefield image, where factory smoke mixes
with the fog of war, indicating the complex mix of
ecological and military catastrophe destroying the
region. Such images are doctored and blurred to
prevent their use by Russian spotters and at the
same time provide an important venue for sharing
the experience of the war and finding some way to
witness and document its carnage.

Kuchanskyi conjectures about the collective
subjectivity that such images might evoke, beyond
their overdetermination through increasingly

groundless colonial imaginaries—in which
Ukraine traditionally figured as a granary for
Europe or a source or transit point of fossil fuels
and not as a site of political self-determination
and subjectivation. To Kuchanskyi, the vibrant
media ecology unleashed by the war offers a
chance to unlearn imperialism collectively and,
possibly, a venue for imagining a future that is
not captured by global war technologies or the
extraction and transportation of oil and gas to
feed Europe's exorbitant energy needs.

It is precisely the link between war and
resource mining that stands at the center of
philosopher Michael Marder's contribution. For
decades, war was outsourced to the world beyond
a prosperous Europe—just like the extraction of
natural resources and its rising human and ecological costs. Now, both are back, with the sudden
blockade of Russian fossil fuels cuing new gas
and shale operations in Western Europe. Marder
considers this new situation through Sigmund
Freud's notion of the return of the repressed. War
and mining are both "dirty affairs" containing and
channeling "raw libidinal forces ... entwined with
large-scale destruction and, in the last instance,
with the death drive." As Marder points out, their
return is no mere repetition. The repressed returns
in a mutated form, as Freud realized, dredging up
many attendant phenomena.

This is why the war in Ukraine reenacts and
unfreezes multiple histories, including the Soviet
collapse, World Wars I and II, the so-called
Russian Civil War after the October Revolution,
the genocidal Holodomor famine, but also
Chernobyl and the coming ecological catastrophe.
As Marder outlines, these multiple histories cave
in under their own weight and implode, unleash-
ing massive centripetal forces. The war shares this
logic with that of the environmental crisis and its
prospect of mass extinction. "The centrality of

fossil fuels to environmental degradation and to the possibilities of funding Putin's regime holds a clue to their cobelonging within the paradigm of the implosion of history," he writes. This paradigm can only be grasped and counteracted with a philosophy of history robust enough to deal with multiple contradictions and complexities as they collide and collapse.

For writer Martin Pollack, the war in Ukraine has prompted the return of old fears and prejudices, blocked out and repressed in the postwar era but also since the end of the Cold War. Pollack recalls just how strongly paternalistic Austria's attitude to Eastern Europe has always been. The Nazi crimes committed there were swept under the rug as the Iron Curtain kept the entire region out of sight and out of mind. This ignorance allows people in Austria and elsewhere to be swayed by Russian propaganda, while knowledge of the current atrocities by Russian soldiers requires an almost moral choice to face up to Europe's complicity in tacitly and even actively supporting Putin's regime.

Pollack tackles one of the central ideological problems of the war—namely, the gulf between the real histories it digs up and the fake histories it projects. This gulf is especially broad in the use of the term "fascism"—the war's central embattled signifier. While the Putin regime's ideology has traits reminiscent of fascism, and its forces behave like fascist occupiers, it tries to disable criticism by claiming to be denazifying Ukraine. Not that anyone would believe this in the end. But the point is to turn fascism into an empty word, to render it ambiguous and unusable.

In her contribution, Marcia Sá Cavalcante Schuback examines this "fascism of ambiguity" as a technique gestating for quite some time in politics and highly visible in the rise of right-wing populists such as Jair Bolsonaro or Donald Trump. It is a new evolution from historical fascism—which in Benito Mussolini's time celebrated heroic death as the highest form of life in service to the fascist community. Neofascism, as defined by Pier Paolo Pasolini, relies rather upon media culture and its atomizing effects; it breaks resistance by disabling the senses and the ability to make sense of the world.

Schuback describes how social media have pushed Pasolini's TV-era neofascism into a new phase. Now, fascism profits from the conditions of a democracy succumbing to algorithms, where the bondless bonds and relationless relations of social media allow meanings to oscillate and become fully ambiguous. This is why Putinist fascists can masquerade as anti-fascists on a mission to "denazify" Ukraine.

What is needed is a mechanism of differentiation, allowing the notion of fascism itself to be recuperated and applied where necessary. Oxana Timofeeva demonstrates how such a recuperation might be effected and brought to bear on Russia's war of aggression and crimes like those in the city of Bucha near Kyiv. To Timofeeva, these present a distorted mirror of what in psychoanalysis is known as the death drive, describing how a subject's self-destructive energies translate into outward aggression.

Timofeeva uses G. W. F. Hegel and Georges Bataille to shed light on this death drive as a collective phenomenon. Its subject is an empire—but one that refuses to follow the idealistic script laid out by Hegel in his seminal *Phenomenology of Spirit*. Here, the empty legalism, social atomization, and potential despotism of large empires would be overcome by revolutions and the resulting "modern" states of mutual recognition. Fascism is a mutation of this path, evidence of a failed revolution. It "functions in accordance with the mechanism that Freud revealed as the death drive at the origins of war: instead of letting itself be demolished by the storm of revolution, a given form of power and property relations calling itself a nation tries to preserve itself and find another object for its (self-)destructive impulses." These self-destructive impulses might also mean something else, namely a limit to an empire's growth. Referring to Bataille, for whom war was the catastrophic result of a social inability to redistribute nonproductively or spend accumulated wealth in any other way than through wholesale destruction, Timofeeva hopes that "what presents itself as an attempt to restore the Russian Empire is in fact the reality of its collapse."

The essays collected in this volume are followed by a selection of literary texts. Two of these are excerpts from works premiered at the festival and relate to the memories and associations the war brings up even from afar. Theatermaker Boris Nikitin's solo piece explores the silence shrouding the story of his Slovakian grandmother, Magda Toffler, who turned out to be Jewish and had spent World War II in hiding. Philosopher and writer Keti Chukhrov's short film revisits the breakaway republic of Abkhazia in Georgia and explores the surreal and broken world inhabited by those who chose to stay in the former war zone.

The final four pieces are a selection of poetry and short prose on the war in Ukraine. They were part of a larger selection published in the well-known Graz-based literary magazine *manuskripte* in collaboration with the festival and appear here in English translation. Syargey Prylutsky's poems describe the experience of survival by chance at the time of the full-fledged invasion. Galina Rymbu imagines war as a monstrous rose at the center of a hellish and strangely ornate landscape. In her prose poem, Dana Kavelina presents a stark vision of Easter resurrection, revealing the ghoulish religious and redemptive narratives and genocidal intentionality mobilized by the Russian campaign. Ostap Slyvynsky's "War Vocabulary" collects stories of ordinary people on streets and shelters throughout Ukraine, presenting a close-up panorama of the war in everyday tales of perseverance and survival.

If one thing becomes clear after reading the contributions, it is that there are ways of combating the paralysis of uncertainty and the seduction of normalcy. The outcome of not only the war in Ukraine but the larger battle against contemporary fascism depends upon not falling back into inaction and intellectual complacency. That is what will make up the history of our uncertain future, no matter how hard the likes of Putin try to rewrite history to turn it into myth. The solidarity, bravery, ingenuity, and humor of ordinary Ukrainians in the face of the seemingly overpowering military machine have revealed that collective agency can overcome the dysfunctional and inhuman force of a rotting empire.

22

I Follow My Future History, I Do Not Know What It Is

Maja Haderlap

23

The history of human cognitive ability is one of
delay, of learning from mistakes and repeated
attempts, a story of insight, delusion, of blindness
even.[1] We do not see clearly, and we experience
the world as we have learned to, as we expect
reality to be.

I place these very condensed anthropological, philosophical findings at the start of my
reflections, knowing that, despite many years of
reading and more than a few life experiences, I can
only comprehend a rather limited part of human
nature. As a writer, one is at best eager to hone
one's perceptiveness and to contextualize plausibly
what is happening in the world. And yet, nowadays
it is becoming ever more difficult to comment
on political, economic, and social conditions or
even to imagine the future. We stand in the midst
of events and often don't know what exactly is
happening. We're surrounded by a seemingly
immeasurable, inescapable confusion of voices
and opinions coming from speakers masquerading
as truth-tellers, orators, warnings, the voice of
the people, rabble-rousers, opinion leaders, and
experts. What could distinguish a writer's voice
from all the others? Can a writer speak differently
or more credibly about our complicated reality, a
reality furthermore that seems to change daily?

I have my doubts, yet I believe that we must
think publicly and join in all the debates we follow
because our work is focused on the fate of human-
kind as a whole. We deploy our languages and our
wavering perceptive faculty—we must be seekers
and thinkers and insistent.

What we can claim with absolute certainty is
that at present our societies are in, to put it mildly,
a colossal upheaval, the consequences of which
we can only guess at. We are missing the criterion
of experience in this transitional process; we are
slipping into the unknown, surrounded by mili-
taristic rhetoric, fear of crises, and chaos. We are

constantly seeking trustworthy, verifiable sources
of knowledge and experience. The situation is
paradoxical. Never before was so much information available to our societies; we are flooded
with an abundance of news, yet still lose our
sense of direction. Innumerable bits of so-called
information turn out, on closer examination, as
we well know, to be informational garbage driven
by an unfettered attention industry based on
algorithms or by particular interests that cannot
be immediately identified. These developments
strike us unprepared, for our general cognitive
ability and our power of judgment, on which we
pride ourselves so greatly, are far from sufficiently
superbly trained.

On occasion, however, drastic events or mis-
fortune befall us in a way that changes our attitude
in a short span of time, and we no longer trust the
old, presumed certainties. Suddenly, we believe
we can recognize things that we previously did not
notice. I would subsume these incisive moments
into the currently topical notion of tipping points.

It is on these tipping points in our approach to
reality that I would like to reflect today.

The expression "tipping point" smells of metal,
doesn't it? It's a term that is now understood
even when it sounds clanging and destructive. It
indicates a rupture, an irreversible moment from
which there is no return to an earlier time, the shift
of an era when past, present, and future coincide
and the future part becomes the present. A term
like an accident.

We try to orient ourselves and turn our eyes to
the future, there, where we are not. We believe we
can see the future far in the distance before it starts
to dawn on us that in the crisis, the future has been
visiting for some time. The future, we secretly feel,
will be our history. "I follow my future history. I do
not know what it is," is stated in the photographer
Susan Meiselas's installation, in which she tracks

the paths of this world's refugees. I have chosen these two sentences as the motto of my lecture.

My talk about the future will, therefore, be a talk about the present, a reflection on our present, which is making us dizzy. The "we" that I'm using refers to that section of the world's population in our rich societies that is using up the bulk of the world's natural resources with their consumer habits. I have slipped behind the mask of an unspecified middle class; my "we" is not identificational, it is variable and directed at the community I know, but not only—a community that gears its lifespan to having a good time and closes its eyes to current violent social upheavals. I'd like to speak about its desire to delay the moment of action, to settle into inertia, and, at worst, to become aggressive, aggressive against everyone and everything that might disturb its narrow self-perception.

How, then, do we imagine the future? Does it only serve as a projection surface that mirrors our desires and fears? For far too long, we have shifted our omissions to the future in order to absolve ourselves from our responsibility in the present.

With remarkable self-aggrandizement, we regard the past as a waste dump in which, at best, we poke around for something useful that we claim can be made productive for today. When we still had some conception of it, the future counted as a place of utopia, hope, and promise: now it has degenerated into a place of apocalypse, a repository for our failed projects. We perceive it as a threat and are paralyzed with fear. Out of expediency, we have agreed to extend the present and center our desires on the so-called moment. Sophisticated, advanced high-speed technologies allow us to effortlessly overcome space, distance, and time. Everything happens *just in time*; even procedures shrink to seconds with the help of technology. We blow the present up to an oversized bubble, which, like all bubbles in this world, can disperse into thin air—for the most part, when reality has a rift and the air escapes from the bubble. Only then do we wake from our state of astonishment.

You know the situation. You begin the day, listen to the news or read the newspaper, skimming reports of wars and catastrophes, which become familiarized like a kind of constant background noise. Sometimes you grow more irritated or discontented, even though the wars and catastrophes are generally taking place far away, in the past, or on another continent. Futurologist voices demanding our trust have long tried to make us believe that wars would forevermore be only distant wars, wars that, thanks to global economic interdependence and technological developments, could even be won from afar, without us having to get our hands dirty, and that such wars always serve freedom and no longer need concern us.

Then a morning comes when a surprise war, completely unexpected even though it has been staged before the eyes of the world, tears us from our half-slumber. You start listening to the news again, checking the Internet, and spending more time in front of the television. Dumbed-down reality, in which we'd long believed ourselves secure, suddenly attacks us, fraught with events that had been coming for us without our previously taking any notice. We might have seen a sign, if we had looked more closely or listened more carefully, but we preferred not to know anything in detail. Suddenly, we feel surrounded and abruptly attacked by something intangible. We're shaken, even though we believe we have everything under control.

Well, we have become rather more nervous—this we admit—and, compared to before, we feel less secure. Maybe the pandemic and its deadly consequences have put us on high alert. Or maybe our alarm comes from suddenly grasping how close a war can sneak up on us, so close that it intrudes on our daily life?

We realize with dismay that people we know, cities and places we may have visited, have been attacked by the powerful army of a plutocrat who was able to hijack an entire nation. We debate the new situation and yet don't hear any bombs exploding. There are no corpses rotting amid rubble in our cities; we have no reason to take refuge in air-raid shelters. We take part in solidarity demonstrations for Ukraine, collect donations, support friends who are in turn supporting friends and people in need. We hope we'll be spared this time as well, that the luck of peace will remain on our side as it has for decades. How much longer? An eternity, a moment? We don't know; we hope and believe and bluster and engage in action as we always do when we feel uncertain and want to take a public stance. At the end of the day, for the sake of normality, we go about our usual business.

Our vision remains clouded though our anxiety has grown. We decide to enjoy the summer and, after the stressful lockdowns, to finally go out among people and into the open air. We lie on the beach, sit in city parks, or walk past withered fields and forests; the sun is shining, and the heat feels like an unrelenting furnace. It seems to come from all sides, from above, from below, from left and right. The heat has an unfamiliar intensity, as if it were accumulating exponentially in the atmosphere, and it expands strangely. We're still prepared to consider it a temporary phenomenon; we listen to the weather forecast and take comfort in predictions of rain. Yes, global warming, yes, yes, climate disaster. At the same time, we've been sorting our recycling for years, buying organic food, consuming sustainably; we've been doing absolutely everything right, but nature won't cooperate. Then the sky grows dark, black thunder clouds gather, a storm, a hurricane breaks out erratically. Branches and halves of trees fly through the neighborhood, windowpanes shatter, roof tiles

rain down, the precipitation is like a dam burst
that sweeps away everything in its path. Houses
and streets and hills and fields, everything is
bearing down on us humans. We rub our eyes and
cannot understand what we see on television, and
yet we calculated everything, we counted on being
spared, we had been assured. We are insured and
confident of victory; we insist on guarantees; we
want our money back. We are convinced of this
until an event strikes us and we are stricken, even
though the majority of us are still spared.

Or we drive to the gas station. The cost of fuel
soars to breathtaking heights, set daily, hourly, by
an automatic algorithm. Unlike us, it leads a life of
its own—the markets, the stock exchanges, we're
told, impossible to intervene in because of their
nature, because of their eternal laws. We spend
hours listening to discussions on television in
which the panelists go round and round in circles.
Many of the reports seem strangely unsatisfying,
in fact, absurd. When they broach the topic of our
trading systems' vulnerability to crises and their
inherent potential dangers, then yes, yes, leftist
squabbling, and we agree with the moderators, and
leave those participants who support an adjust-
ment—or, God forbid, regulation—of the markets
standing there foolishly, as if they had broken a
taboo. The markets and their stakeholders lay low,
avoid all discussions, and have no recognizable
face. Occasionally, a spokesperson will step into
the limelight—men, for the most part—and speak
in the name of the financial, energy, and commodities markets. They speak in coded, dogmatic
phrases that observe reality as if behind a thick
pane of glass, with no access to it. In the belly of the
market, a merciless ideology rules, while outside
bare life seeks a foothold.

A semiconscious state still dominates; the
searing, existential pain that could throw us back
on ourselves has not yet set in; everything still seems

packed in cotton wool. The good old routines of work life, of consumption, still suggest as much as ever the disposability of the world, the disposability of everything and everyone, although we don't see it so narrowly and are fundamentally different. We still believe we can choose, true to the motto *I choose a brand, therefore I am.* What we purchase, what trips we take, multiplies and expands us in a marvelous way. We cannot get enough of ourselves and our potential. Happiness economics takes care of that, helping us feel better in times of crisis through its ingenious methods of suggestion and perhaps responsible, at most, for our personal failures, but not for the state of the world. Happiness is, indeed, often long in coming and is a rare commodity, which distresses us but does not leave us without hope. We try to cure our enfeebled, sickly nature, and spend enormous sums of money on nutritional supplements, psychotropic drugs, painkillers, and opiates. We hope that we've been prescribed the most effective cures and tortures to improve our health and readiness for work as well as our appearance. After waking from a refreshing sleep, we want to find the world and our optimized bodies in a better state and not have to grapple with calamities, illnesses, the hazards of poverty, war, or life's other lethal challenges, and most definitely not with our responsibility for the crisis, the climate, democracy under threat, the abysmal economy, for shambolic politics and weakened institutions, which we, incidentally, have badmouthed along with the neoliberal prophets of our time. Besides, we have no time—the more time we gain and save with the help of accelerating technologies, the greater our time pressure. No seminar on how to slow down can satisfy us, no yoga technique can sufficiently calm us down, no Slow Food can sate us for long.

We believe assiduously that unregulated, market-driven individualism will liberate us and, in order to protect ourselves against the dangers

threatening us from the external world, we drive
ever larger, gas-guzzling, bulky automobiles
that look like tanks or attack dogs crouching to
pounce with bared radiator grills. These giant cars
keep everything at a distance. They obstruct the
sight of children and other drivers, of everything
that creeps and crawls on the ground, while the
occupants of the all-inclusive interiors believe
themselves safe. Not only in America, but here,
too, people are arming themselves privately and
building personal armories, acting warlike, as if
they were living in dangerous, barbaric times in
which one must fight for survival, and it is better to
attack than debate.

The schema of war is omnipresent, not just in
the current clearly militarily led wars. We must
ask ourselves if, given the heightened security
measures in Western societies following 9/11
and the widespread private use of sophisticated
military surveillance technologies, we are not
all engaged in a more or less disguised imitation
war, and if the war does not, in fact, represent, as
my esteemed colleague Franz Schuh put it in an
interview, a kind of late-capitalist industry.[2]

But back to tipping points. Did our eyes open
wide in the moment of fear, did we wake from the
doze into which we were lulled by the addictive
goods of fleeting happiness and personal enhance-
ment ("I decide who I want to be")? Maybe we
thought we could feel the world passing through
a few tipping points while we lay half-asleep.
Tipping points in climate events, tipping points
in environmental pollution, tipping points in the
organization of the global economy, tipping points
in public discourse, which has degenerated into a
slugfest. The ethnologist Hans Peter Duerr writes
that we experience the constant sensory bombard-
ment imposed on us by our lifestyle as a flooding
of our consciousness. This flood overtaxes us and
impedes our ability to distinguish the essential

from the insignificant. With this, we lose part of
our capacity to orient ourselves mentally, morally,
and socially, a capacity on which we are more
dependent than ever before.

I assume, purely hypothetically, that we have,
in the meantime, woken up and remain caught
in a moment of absolute powerlessness. At the
same time, it's dawning on us that we must act.
Basically, we would be prepared to respond to
climate change by changing our energy sources
and adjusting our lifestyle. We'd want to adapt and
change some aspects of our daily lives, but there
are fears, financial constraints, too little that is
tangible, concrete, proven. We sense that we are
dependent on help, cooperation, and encourage-
ment, on constructive examples and collaboration
on the part of everyone in every social sector.
The diktat of endless economic growth and the
relentless global competition that we are injected
with are mechanisms that not only weaken social
cohesiveness in our societies but also siphon
off the planet's resources until the bitter end.
Human and ecological imperatives erode under
the pressure of circumstances. What we need
at this moment are other qualities and skills, a
taste for collaboration, a willingness to share, for
example. How else do we expect to transition to
cleaner, autarkic energy and to establish a food
system that is healthy both for humans and the
ecosystem to the benefit of all? Do we actually
believe that only the rich are entitled to vital and
life-sustaining business practices and not others?

Inflation and price increases put pressure
on us, just as the state is under pressure from all
sides to prevent crises. The conversion to clean
energy will be very costly, we are told by those
who spread doom and gloom when the coffers
are full. One could be forgiven for thinking that
decreasing carbon dioxide emissions is not as
much of a political priority as the survival of fossil

fuel giants and the fossil energy markets. The
struggle over this market has been fiercer and more
relentless than that over changes in our energy and
agricultural systems—even before Russia's invasion
of Ukraine. Conversion is constantly blocked,
impeded, dismissed, delayed—you know, the war,
the war, the effected investments. The fossil empires
(owned in great number, incidentally, by plutocrats
and autocrats) fight back, and not simply this
year alone. They are ready, with delaying tactics,
with extortion, with inflated prices, and with a
flood of digital and analog media, to destabilize
our democracies and public discourse. They have
a record of success, that's undeniable. It's as if
we're being pursued by our own demons, which we
had taken for lucky talismans. We encounter our
mistakes, our own shortcomings, our own ghosts,
and we react overwhelmed, close to chucking it all
in. This is, no doubt, the most dangerous point, the
decisive tipping point after our awakening. Just
now, in Austria, it is being suggested that we will
freeze, even go hungry, that we'll ride out the winter
only with shivering limbs, as if we lived in one of the
poorest nations in the world, where there truly is
nothing to eat and climate change has made entire
regions and countries unlivable. We resist; we've
had our fill of fear-mongering propaganda; we
don't want to hear it anymore, so we think about a
second garage and the next vacation on Rhodes or
in the Maldives, as long as they're still above water.
We console ourselves with sustainable products
that have multiplied like magic on store shelves.
Perhaps we believe since we're realizing that, first
and foremost, this doesn't affect us as much as
others who live elsewhere or who will live after us,
and only subsequently will it affect us, but we could
be mistaken, as we always have been.

Now the moment has come when I should risk
saying "I," a moment when I feel I'm treading on
precarious terrain, because the world's unsolved

problems have grown and not just during the
time that I've been writing this. They oppress us,
and yet the real world remains distanced from us
beyond our consumption. My daily consideration
of how one can, as a single individual, as a writer,
effect any change in the state of the world felt
and still can feel like a roller coaster. My mood
changed hourly. Moments of optimism were
followed by phases of bitterness, in which I was
convinced, looking at global politics, that our
human—or should I say patriarchal—late-capitalist condition opposes our own survival. I admit
that in recent years, shivers ran down my spine
when I read a brilliantly expressed swan song
for an antiquated humanity that has outlived its
day. Nothing conjures up intellectual agitation
as speedily as our well-thought-out will to power
and death drive and the irritating specter of a
technological, posthuman society. Tabula rasa all
around; we would finally be freed from ourselves
and our flaws. If you were to oppose it by arguing
for the quality and miracle of life, you'd find
yourself in unknown waters, in the realm of the
social, the ethical-moral, in domains that we have
successfully removed from public debates and
abandoned to fundamentalist, ideological, and
religious zealots.

At the same time, I realize that not only
problems, but also the archive of knowledge and
restorative, workable ideas is expanding, and yet
I ask myself why thinking about life, death, and
nature seems so difficult and toxic, as if it entailed
a dispute over ownership, as if nothing belonged
to us anymore. We must write and speak about
it so that we don't lose the right to, because it,
too, can be taken from us, as we are coming to
recognize in the increasingly repressive, polar-
ized, misogynist political currents of our time.
Significantly, those who espouse these politics are
all champions of fossil power.

As soon as I say "I," I step into time, into the time that is available to me. A time that is measured not only in hours, days, and years, but also in phases, in developments and cycles. My mortal body is bound to the rhythms of nature. All processes of development take time; little can be accomplished overnight. I need only think of how long it takes for people to work through the trauma of war or historical enmities and prejudices, and it becomes clear that a fixation on the moment makes everything grind to a halt. We stand in a series of developments and, naturally, can shape them, each in his or her particular area. We should all adapt our actions and productions, our daily activities, to the requirements of ecological and economic change—it is in this that I see our responsibility.

We are always and at all times in transition, in flux, not at the end, not only in the present day. Augustine of Hippo, an avowed sinner before his Lord, once wrote that it is not the times that are bad, but our actions, and "we ourselves are the times."[3]

Translated from the German by Tess Lewis

1 Opening speech held at Out
   of Joint—the literary festival
   within steirischer herbst,
   October 11, 2022, Literaturhaus
   Graz. The title quotes Susan
   Meiselas's photography
   project *akaKURDISTAN*,
   March 2019, c/o Berlin.
2 Franz Schuh, "Franz Schuh:
   'Krieg ist spätkapitalistische
   Industrie,'" interview by Ronald
   Pohl, *Der Standard*, July 9,
   2022, https://www.derstandard.
   at/story/2000137298113/
   philosoph-franz-schuh-krieg-ist-
   spaetkapitalistische-industrie,
   accessed November 2, 2022.
3 *The Works of Saint Augustine: A
   Translation for the 21st Century*,
   part 3, vol. 3, *Sermons 51–94*,
   trans. Edmund Hill, ed. John E.
   Rotelle et al. (New York: New
   City Press, 1991), p. 356.

Between Smoke Screen and Blur: Visual Practices in the War Ecology of (Geo)Political Imagination

Olexii Kuchanskyi

39

Figure 1

Russian missile attack on Kremenchug,
April 24, 2022. Source: Trukha ⚡Ukraine
(Telegram channel)

What does the picture in figure 1 imply? To whom is it addressed? One might consider it a kind of portrait of the global network of extraction and sale of resources—the smoke from an explosion is intertwined with that from a factory chimney due to obvious laws of physics. For the cold sky above the building that was hit by a Russian missile, the origin of the smoke does not matter: the temperature of the air, its chemical composition, that is enough for production and war to merge into a single smoke screen over the city.

The source of this image is the Trukha ⚡ Ukraine Telegram channel, a communication platform where the photos of Russian missile attacks and their aftermath are posted. Eyewitnesses of bombings provide administrators of the channel with photo and video content, which later passes a brief check for compliance with martial law and appears online. As the air raid sirens sound, millions of eyes are glued to their screens with thoughts of loved ones, family, and friends across the country. Although Trukha ⚡ Ukraine sometimes publishes unreliable information, the channel is still incredibly popular—like a horoscope or an online tarot reading, it soothes or articulates anxiety with a small image: through its mediation, uncertainty swirls in a vortex or a funnel arising at the site of a rocket explosion.

The lower part of the photo is blurred. This is due to martial law requirements: photo or video documentation of missile strikes can be used by the occupying forces to correct subsequent fire. However, the image still finds its addressee, because a person who is well acquainted with the depicted place can recognize it by secondary features. The channel administrators do not indicate the exact location of the missile attack; they only sometimes mention the area of the city. Instead, the audience localizes it, comparing what they see with memories and associations. For

some, these entanglements serve as an impetus
for evacuating close ones as soon as possible, for
others, to help those who suffer the consequences
of shelling. Tons of spontaneously collected
humanitarian aid, volunteer expeditions, decisions
by political elites, all these phenomena are each
in their own way moderated by images: imprints
still worth recognizing. "Am I correctly identifying
this place?" The imagination intertwines with
associations, a public place with a private memory,
anxiety with hope. This is how the collective body
absorbs the digital image.

What is the agency of such images? How do
they shape subjectivity? It is in the very nature of
images that they operate in the ecology of imagination. Imagination, namely the imagination of the
future activated by collective action, is a key issue
today, especially in Eastern Europe. Meanwhile,
in the West, heads of state to left-wing theorists
and activist movements lack an imaginary of the
future as anything other than a gradual drowning
in Vladimir Putin's repressions or, in contrast, a
future without Putinism as global US hegemony.
Meanwhile, the bodies of people here in Ukraine
are imagined as passive matter—a medium for
the decisions of major geopolitical players. This
imagination is actualized in the lack of weapons
parity and the resulting unequal positions,
which make any kind of negotiation impossible.
Such conditions lead to extremely brutal forms
of warfare, including the death of thousands
of civilians and the destruction of the cities of
Mariupol, Kharkiv, Bucha, Irpin, Mykolayiv, and
Izyum, among many others. It is also reflected in
Ukraine's growing foreign debt. This bill will have
to be footed by the country's lower social strata,
who have suddenly become an extra element in the
political and financial network of Russian gas and
oil distribution. Imagination, that is, abstraction
that materializes in practices, is political. This is

precisely what determines the form of this article—a mental experiment unfolding against the background of images.

The Geopolitics of Groundless Empire

The first step is to imagine the place of events, the environment in which images are incorporated into geopolitical processes. In his essay "Toward Perpetual Peace," Immanuel Kant describes the space of geopolitics as a sphere—a single and universal place of equality between people and their natural right to any part of the planet. However, the fact that every person has the right to any place on Earth also means that no one has the right to encroach on another's place. Therefore, "perpetual peace," according to Kant, would be guaranteed by institutional restrictions such as borders, nations, et cetera.[1] The only thing that casts doubt on this idyllic, homely story is that, in addition to its spherical shape, the Earth also has unevenly distributed deposits of substances, better known as natural resources. It is precisely this circumstance that provokes the political imagination to "clarify" and redraw the lines on the globe time after time in spite of perpetual peace (see fig. 2).

Ryan Bishop points out that the ways in which political agency is imagined are crucial to grasping the ways of policing the Earth, that is, geopolitics itself. This has certainly been the case since the Cold War, as Bishop states, when teletechnology became involved in the process of imagining the world and humanity's place in it. The screen image encodes the ways in which the self relates to objects (and other subjects) in the world as what Bishop calls a "subject of mastery," controlling and destroying objects from afar.[2] New imaging technologies suggest the planetary perspective of a (geo) political imagination. This reflects the challenges

43

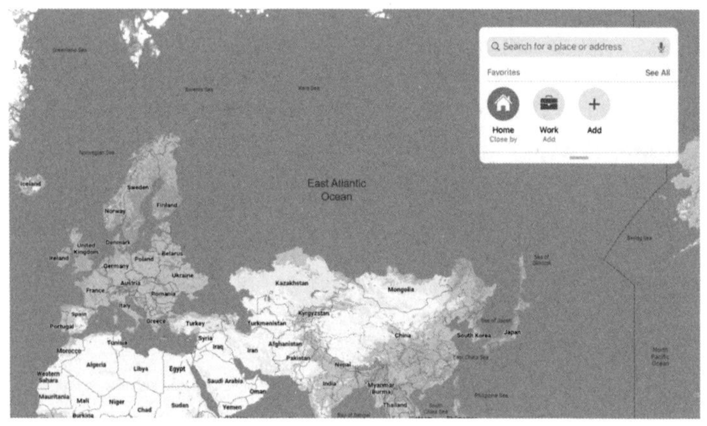

Figure 2

"Russia Removed from Apple Maps,"
The Babylon Bee, March 4, 2022,
https://babylonbee.com/news/
russia-removed-from-apple-maps

"CUPERTINO, CA—In an unprecedented effort to put additional pressure on Russia, Apple Inc. has announced they will be removing the entire country from Apple maps."

associated with humanity's ability not only to influence geological processes but to even perceive nature as structured data. Moreover, our time has seen the collapse of what Carl Schmitt called "the *nomos* of the earth,"[3] modernity's persistent idea that the world and nature itself require resource extraction, the subjugation of indigenous peoples, and colonial expansion. As Tony Fry and Madina Tlostanova write, two world wars and anti-colonial movements present a clear verdict on such a "*nomos*."[4] Hence, (geo)political imaginaries privatized by various mass media companies are now open to the most determined delusions. Moreover, these delusions are usually gathered from and haunted by old nightmares. In the following, I will focus on the colonial imaginings that surround the formation of the territory of today's Ukraine.

At the outset of Russia's full-scale invasion of Ukraine, when air raids were especially massive and Russian forces were attempting to surround Kyiv, Asia Bazdyrieva observed how these territories were being reinscribed and remapped by Western geography and geology.[5] The history of rendering Eastern European land as a resource dump reaches to the Renaissance (whence the birth of capitalism), when previous suppliers of grain (Greece, Thrace, and Egypt) became subjects of the Ottoman Empire. It was then that the "outskirts of Europe" came to occupy a key place in food trade chains.

The culture of Romanticism made many efforts to exoticize the fertile "granary of Europe," creating conditions for a far less romantic "steel fever" in the 19th century. During this period, key centers of resource extraction took shape on the territory of modern Ukraine, attracting a great deal of Russian and European capital. In particular, this gave rise to the mining town of Yuzivka (Hughsivka), named after the Welsh entrepreneur John James Hughes— today this town is called Donetsk, and after 2014 it became known worldwide due to its occupation by the Russian Federation, which created a puppet republic there. The western part of Ukraine, formerly Galicia, was part of the Austro-Hungarian Empire. It too was developed as a resource dump in the 19th century, as Alison Fleig Frank has shown. Until World War I, Austria-Hungary was among the five largest oil-producing regions largely because of Galicia's oil fields.[6]

Later, the formation of Soviet biopolitics significantly shaped the current situation of Ukraine. It was in the 1930s, Bazdyrieva states, that the body of the "Enemy of the People" was formed. This body's punishment, if spared execution, was exile to Kolyma or other places with strategic concentrations of gold, tin, and diamond deposits for the Soviet economy.[7] Obviously, no less strategic was the unpaid labor of those who insisted on more democratic forms of socialism and wider autonomy of the republics, critics of Joseph Stalin's deviation from Vladimir Lenin's course, or even simply those who fell under planned repressions—as is known, Stalinism gave birth to some of the most brutal and exploitative forms of slave labor under the auspices of planned economy and prisoner reeducation. According to Bazdyrieva, what unites these different historical forms of the colonial imagination is the *desubjectivation* of Ukrainian bodies. On the cognitive map of modernity, they appear as little more than inert matter, requiring the intervention of an external subject.

Another aspect of today's (geo)political imaginary and the rendering-passive of Ukrainian subjects, bodies, and land is Ukraine's role as a transit point for resources. Oleksiy Radynski describes the impact of gas agreements between West Germany and the USSR, which resulted in the construction of two major pipelines on Ukrainian territory.[8]

Since the 1990s, (geo)political imaginations appropriated by private mass media have built a sort of social delirium around these objects of natural-resource extraction and transit. Political talk shows have affirmed the strength of Europe's economic alliance with the Russian Federation, while historical TV shows about World War II have highlighted Russia's heroic role in liberating the world from Nazism (although Ukrainians, Belarusians, and representatives of other Soviet republics fought on the side of the USSR to no small extent). Even before the full-scale invasion of Ukraine, the more sophisticated newspaper columns were making extensive arguments about why it is impossible for Western countries to embargo Russian fuel.[9] Against the background of such an imagination pumped up with Siberian gas, even the most radical leftist critics assert that subjectivity in geopolitical processes can be localized on both sides of the pipelines, while they doubt that it can exist in the space they extend over—that is, in the form of popular action in Ukraine.[10]

Faced with the transformation of Ukrainian political life in the direction of greater autonomy from the Russian Federation, Russian political and economic elites have always responded with the "gas argument." Thus, after the Orange Revolution of 2004, when the Ukrainian people refused to recognize the falsified electoral victory of pro-Putin presidential candidate Viktor Yanukovych, Gazprom refused to supply the gas agreed upon when the more loyal Leonid Kuchma was still in power.[11] In 2014, a sudden change in course from EU integration to a more pro-Russian stance sparked the popular uprising called Maidan. The Russian state reacted by occupying Crimea, and later, in March 2020, by capturing the facilities of the largest gas and oil production company on the Black Sea, Chornomornaftogaz, by military force as well.[12] Places with some of the highest concentrations of likely shale deposits in Ukraine were occupied— including the Yuzivska gas field in the Donbas.

At first glance, the "blitzcringe" of Putin's troops in the winter of 2022 (the intention to occupy Ukraine within three days) might seem absurd, but, suddenly, it does not seem so groundless. Obviously, in addition to oil and gas, there are many other reasons for the occupation of Crimea, the hybrid war in Donbas, and the full-scale invasion. It is impossible to list them all. I propose to keep in mind the conditioning of these processes by colonial patterns of (geo)political imagination and the subordinate inclusion of Ukraine in the extraction and production of mined goods. Separately, I want to emphasize the importance of teletechnological images—the main medium of transnational Putinist gaslighting. Its primary means are gas blackmail, manipulating the memory of World War II, preemptive attacks on imagined threats like the expansion of NATO or "Gayrope" through Ukraine, as well as the constant labeling of any attempts by Ukrainians to acquire a nation-state as Nazism.

It is striking that precisely these imaginaries found such a wide response with both Russian and Western European audiences and not, say, assumptions about Ukraine's will to political self-determination (*auto-nomia*), or the memory of how many Ukrainians lost their lives in the war on Nazism. For the colonized political imagination, any fiction seems more convincing than the assumption of the subjectivity of "inert matter," that is, of the periphery from the point of view of the metropolis. As said before, these processes take place against the background of privatized imaginaries and a globally unsettled relationship between self and Earth—the collapse of the "*nomos*" of Western knowledge, previously claimed to be "universal" and subjecting surrounding cultures to epistemological colonization for over five centuries.

Mercury determines the course of the ongoing war in Ukraine no less than Mars. Indeed, this set

of events can be imagined as a node of interrelated
kinetic processes, which are not determined by a
single ideological frame, but rather emerge at the
intersection of labor extraction, fossil resources,
market and warfare processes, as well as the privatization of geopolitical imaginations.

Images and the In_Formation of Value

Figure 3 is a screenshot of a mobile app that warns
Ukrainians about incoming air raids. The air defense
system predicts the trajectory of a missile, so only
residents of certain parts of the country will receive
notifications. This screenshot was taken after the
threat, so the screen says "no alarm." A strange
coincidence, very revealing in our case: in Ukrainian
the equivalent of "air alarm" is *povitriana tryvoha*,
literally "air anxiety." The image is minimal, limited
to text and color (red: there is an alarm, blue: there is
none). Yet it informs not only the mental state of the
population but also their behavior; institutions and
businesses must close during an air alarm, which in
turn sets off further warnings in the financial sphere
or other social sectors. Each alarm is accompanied
by a surge of anger and hatred toward the Russian
Federation; that is, it provokes a violent pulsation of
the (geo)political imagination.
　　These notifications might lead us to consider
further aspects of the agency of images: their
impact upon the in_formation of value. What is
specific about popular images is their capacity to
inform. This statement may seem too simple and
obvious if one does not clarify the meaning of
the term "information." In the literal sense, it is a
process that gives something a form, "in-forms" it.
I call this the "in_formation of value" (not just the
formation), bearing in mind the important difference between these processes and similar patterns
of economic life in the industrial age.

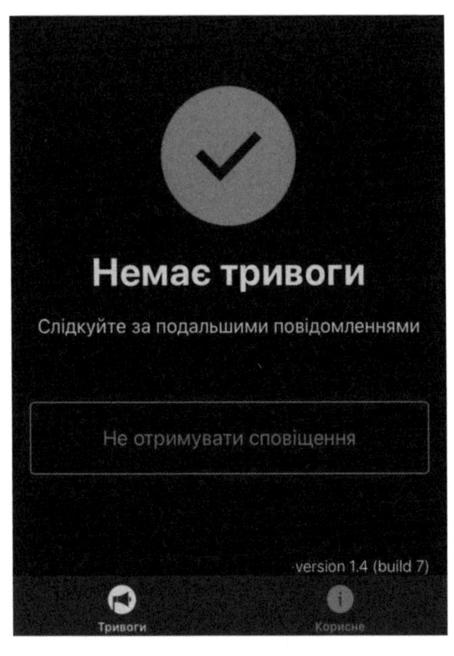

Figure 3

Screenshot of Povitriana tryvoha, a Ukrainian
mobile app that warns of incoming air raids

50

Obviously, images play a key role in this in_formation of value for at least two reasons: first, in the age of excess data ("Big Data"), visual media prevail over many others in terms of the speed of communication; second, as media theorist Laura U. Marks has observed, the practices of seeing have always been central to other practices of comprehension in Western culture.[13] In_formation of value is a nonlinear process that requires value to not only be formed by informational means but also constantly updated by new information reaching the audience (customers). The activities of users in social networks and on the Internet in general, today's medical science, and the data collected by advertising companies and national governments have created the conditions for the birth of what Zach Blas calls "the Quantified Self"—a self as a structure of data.[14] Collective or individual subjectivities in such conditions become more predictable and controllable than ever before— capital and the state surely take advantage of this. Images themselves are agents of in_formation: they operate within the affective economy. This, in turn, involves a great deal of unpaid labor and the instrumentalization of sentiments—considered a new resource. Finally, such a system can only exist through a new form of power, based upon preemptive planning vis-à-vis risk, only possible by creating a climate of ubiquitous anxiety and constructing threats to be preempted.

Studies of digital capitalism have repeatedly emphasized how user-generated data is used to form a more attractive product. Henry Jenkins points out that neither marketers nor AI ad services actually produce affects. Instead, they mobilize and assemble existing affects using the "raw material" obtained from "sentiment analysis." The historical and cultural novelty of such an analysis of feelings is that, unlike ideology, it does not produce a field of relatively stable truths for the community. Instead, it attracts and, through marketing, multiplies the community's eclectic judgments and internal contradictions as well as the consumers' pseudo-truths. Marketing and advertising form an interactive environment of consumption and data extraction, which Jenkins calls a "convergent culture," that is, a culture where nominal consumers of products participate in production no less than nominal producers ("prosumption").[15]

Nowhere is this clearer than in what images do to spectators, manipulating and triggering preexisting affects, such as the desire for security or fulfillment and the fear of loss. Such reactions to images clearly add to the in_formation of value. Jason W. Moore argues that value is not only the average labor time embedded in a commodity but always generated at the expense of what he calls "Cheap Nature"—the essentialized labor of nonhumans, free reproductive labor (usually carried out by women), and the labor of colonized peoples.[16] Not only the activity of Internet users and TV audiences but also the theft and export of Ukrainian grain to the Russian Federation, the coercion of people in the occupied territories to clean up rubble in exchange for humanitarian aid, and the occupation of foreign territories to prevent economic losses in the global fossil market—all these practices widely used by Russia today can be considered forms of value formation at the expense of Cheap Nature.

How such practices influence power relations was famously discussed by Brian Massumi. In analyzing the so-called politics of fear of the Bush administration's War on Terror, Massumi investigates "ontopower," a new regime of power relations by and large based on administering affects.[17] The well-known events of 9/11 and the Bush administration's "preempting" of any number of perceived threats instituted a climate of public paranoia

focused on terrorism, which itself is poorly understood, as Massumi argues.[18] It denotes phenomena
that are not so much observed as imaginary, actual
as potential, risks rather than certitudes.

It doesn't take long to understand that
Russian propaganda is an analogue of the Bush
administration's politics of fear, mobilizing
the same affects with "Ukrainian Nazism,"
"extremism," "gay propaganda," and "NATO
expansion." Western Europeans in turn worry
about "escalation" with semi-indifference, while
EU governments build their foreign policies on
its prevention and left-wing criticism focuses on
NATO and the Washington Consensus.

Unlearning Imperialism

What agency can images have in such economies
of affect and regimes of ontopower? What forms
of counterpower can they attain? The image in
figure 4 was produced by the Freefilmers collective,
who have been supplying occupied cities with
medicine almost since the beginning of the full-
scale invasion, as well as bringing food, hygiene
products, power generators, and emergency
medical supplies into the vicinity of occupied
territories. The activists' faces are hidden for
security reasons. The collective involves an international network of fellows with skills acquired
in the process of film production: fundraising and
logistics—used, for example, to organize charity
screenings for the benefit of the Freefilmers' volunteer activities. None of this explains why an image
meant to provide information about the transfer
of humanitarian aid looks excessively decorative.
What kind of affective self-governance and
in_formation of value is introduced by such visual
practices? To align one's own imagination with
this image, I propose to look at various historical
precedents of the convergence of visual practices

53

Figure 4

Freefilmers, artist and activist NGO. Source:
Instagram (@freefilmers.ua)

with war as they appear in the theory and criticism of visual culture.

Paul Virilio has shown how perceptual technologies used by military aviation and reconnaissance (remote vision, radars, sensors, et cetera) have replaced the homogeneity of vision on the battlefield, mediated exclusively by human eyes, with the heterogeneity of operational perceptual fields.[19] This has created the conditions for what filmmaker and critic of visual culture Harun Farocki calls the "operational image": visual noise for the human eye that is at the same time meaningful data for military equipment.[20] But what happens if a viewer (or a user) appears in an image's operational field? Can a lived experience be part of an assemblage together with perceptual technologies and the in_formation of value (which, as indicated above, is closely related to processes of war)?

The flickering multiplicity of experiences inhabiting the image adds something superfluous to war images. The Freefilmers' image and the first figure of this text are mirror images and can be considered as visual articulations of the ecstatic (dividual) subjectivity by itself. Their articulation goes beyond the operation of in_formation due to its own "imperfection," profane and incompetent in affect management, pragmatically open to uncertain scenarios of the future.

Ariella Aïsha Azoulay embeds the agency of images into the larger context of imperialism and colonialism, which shapes its subjects through the very act of vision.[21] Curator and theorist Doreen Mende conjugates this approach with that of Farocki's operative image and examines the capacity of the image to "unlearn imperialism." Unlearning decomposes the homogeneity of the world as it appears in the colonial imagination into the heterogeneity of worlds; the image as abstraction is a world-making device, which requires sociability, interaction between an image and its surroundings.[22] As in the first figure of this article and the last one, images require a reaction: becoming aware of missile attacks without spreading secret information or supporting a transnational network of volunteer initiatives. Such visual expressions of collective ecstatic subjectivity have become a reference for the (geo)political imaginations of political assemblies, who now face Russian colonial violence in the form of political, economic, or epistemic inequality in the entire former Soviet space as well as in feminist, queer, and indigenous communities in the Russian Federation. Some of these visual practices are linked to the political praxis of wider anti-globalist, leftist, and feminist communities, who resist complex forms of oppression, just as in the case of Ukraine, where dependence on the global Western financial market is intertwined with Russian cultural and military colonial violence.

The question is how this collective subjectivity can be installed in and infect a larger field of social practices so that it will not be captured by neoliberal cycles of capital accumulation and domestication of popular political agency by subjectivizing the self as an atomized individual. In times of open warfare, it seems that both these political options depend on something close to what Aristotle calls *zōē*—the very frame of political life, that is, existence itself. Here, my mental experiment must end with a certain degree of opacity. The future can either be imagined as captured by global war technologies, with any alternative forms of common action annihilated by imperial means of repression. Or it can provoke imaginaries of the geopolitical state where a node of the global extractivist order may reach the point of bifurcation. This would not only involve a larger political and social turbulence but the opacity of multiple futures. Although the second scenario does not necessarily lead to emancipation, it is marked by

the constant opacity to potential bifurcations of
the extractivist order and its horizon. Perhaps that
is what this text is rehearsing. While intelligent
theoretical discourse on this war is overrated, its
future depends no less upon military equipment
and operations than upon their epistemic milieu.

1 Immanuel Kant, "Toward Perpetual Peace: A Philosophical Sketch," in *Toward Perpetual Peace and Other Writings on Politics, Peace, and History*, ed. Pauline Kleingeld, trans. David L. Colclasure (New Haven, CT: Yale University Press, 2006), pp. 67–109.

2 Ryan Bishop, "Geopolitics," in *Posthuman Glossary*, ed. Rosi Braidotti and Maria Hlavajova (London: Bloomsbury, 2018), pp. 182–84.

3 Carl Schmitt, *The Nomos of the Earth in the International Law of the Jus Publicum Europaeum*, trans. G. L. Ulmen (New York: Telos, 2006).

4 Tony Fry and Madina Tlostanova, *A New Political Imagination: Making the Case* (London: Routledge, 2020), pp. 107–10.

5 Asia Bazdyrieva, "No Milk, No Love," *E-Flux Journal*, May 2022, https://www.e-flux.com/journal/127/465214/no-milk-no-love/, accessed October 28, 2022.

6 Alison Fleig Frank, *Oil Empire: Visions of Prosperity in Austrian Galicia* (Cambridge, MA: Harvard University Press, 2007), p. 4.

7 Asia Bazdyrieva, "Ukraina y Antropocen: Zemlia," *Korydor*, December 18, 2020, http://www.korydor.in.ua/ua/stories/ukraine-antropocen.html, accessed October 28, 2022.

8 Oleksiy Radynski, "Is Data the New Gas?," *E-Flux Journal*, March 2020, https://www.e-flux.com/journal/107/322782/is-data-the-new-gas/, accessed October 28, 2022.

9 "How Will Europe Cope If Russia Cuts off Its Gas?," *The Economist*, January 29, 2022, https://www.economist.com/europe/2022/01/29/how-will-europe-cope-if-russia-cuts-off-its-gas, accessed November 23, 2022—published nearly a month before the full-scale invasion.

10 See, e.g., Maurizio Lazzarato, "War, Capitalism, Ecology: Why Can't Bruno Latour Understand Anything about Them?," Ill Will, April 4, 2022, https://illwill.com/war-capitalism-ecology, accessed July 5, 2022.

11 The chronology of events is reconstructed here, while interpretations should be revised: Jim Nichol, Steven Woehrel, and Bernard A. Gelb, *Russia's Cutoff of Natural Gas to Ukraine: Context and Implications*, Congressional Research Service report no. RS22378 (2006).

12 "Russia Operates Captured Ukrainian Oil Rigs in Ukraine's Exclusive Economic Zone," InformNapalm, March 28, 2020, https://informnapalm.org/en/russia-operates-captured-ukrainian-oil-rigs-in-ukraines-exclusive-economic-zone/, accessed July 5, 2022.

13 Laura U. Marks, *The Skin of the Film: Intercultural Cinema, Embodiment, and the Senses* (Durham, NC: Duke University Press, 2000), pp. 130–32.

14 Zach Blas, "Information Opacity," in *Posthuman Glossary*, ed. Rosi Braidotti and Maria Hlavajova (London: Bloomsbury, 2018), pp. 198–99.

15 Henry Jenkins, "Buying into *American Idol*: How We Are Being Sold on Reality TV," in *Convergence Culture: Where Old and New Media Collide* (New York: New York University Press, 2006), pp. 59–92.

16 Jason W. Moore, *Capitalism in the Web of Life: Ecology and the Accumulation of Capital* (London: Verso, 2015), pp. 61–64.

17 Brian Massumi, *Ontopower: War, Powers, and the State of Perception* (Durham, NC: Duke University Press, 2015).

18 Ibid., pp. 12–15.

19 Paul Virilio, *War and Cinema: The Logistics of Perception*, trans. Patrick Camiller (London: Verso, 2009), pp. 22–27.

20 This notion was developed through the filmmaker's trilogy *Eye/Machine* (2001–03) and has already become a topic of several theoretical investigations.

21 Ariella Aïsha Azoulay, *Potential History: Unlearning Imperialism* (London: Verso, 2019).

22 Doreen Mende, "The Code of Touch: Navigating Beyond Control, or, Towards Scalability and Sociability," *E-Flux Journal*, May 2020, https://www.e-flux.com/journal/109/331193/the-code-of-touch-navigating-beyond-control-or-towards-scalability-and-sociability/, accessed October 28, 2022.

The Return of the Repressed and the Implosion of History

Michael Marder

61

Twenty twenty-two will be remembered as the year when the repressed returned to Europe. As always, the repressed did not return alone; its comeback was double—and in this doubling, with its countless speculative mirroring effects, we may already discern the interplay of a multiplicity, of the many that inhabit the space and the time between two. War and mining surfaced again in Europe, just when it appeared that they were gone for good, done and over with at the dusk of the 20th century.

Actually, neither activity had been really dispensed with; like much of the material production of our reality, they had been merely outsourced to other parts of the world, whether to Africa or the Middle East or Asia. From their relative concealment, war and mining had been reliably yielding their devastating fruit: leveled mountains, destroyed ecosystems and cities, piled-up corpses of soldiers and, increasingly, civilians caught in the crosshairs of armed conflicts. The fires of explosions and industrial furnaces burnt elsewhere, guaranteeing relatively clean, breathable air for Europe. Their displacement was also behind the illusion of European calm, of the technocratic cooling down of the Western body politic, of voter apathy and civic disengagement, further intensified by the pandemic (the fight against which, incidentally, was labeled by political leaders all over the world as "being at war with a virus"). Perhaps only populist movements on the extreme right kept the illusion of political risk in the electoral process, replayed ad nauseum, with limited success, both in Europe and in the United States.

In fact, the repressed had been barely repressed, given the incursions of Vladimir Putin's army into Georgia in 2008 and into Ukraine in 2014, military operations that resulted in the separation of South Ossetia and Abkhazia from Georgia, the annexation of Crimea by the Russian Federation, and unrest in the Donbas region, a traditional coal-mining and steel-manufacturing area. The same is true with regard to the so-called green energy transition that centers on the rejection of fossil fuels (coal, crude oil, natural gas) while embracing environmentally damaging practices, such as the cultivation of monocultures for the purpose of distilling biodiesel from corn or sugar cane. All too often, marketing strategies, such as selling electric cars and similar "zero-emissions" contrivances, occlude both the sources of electricity powering them and the lithium mining necessary to produce the batteries for this storing of energy. In 2020, roughly 80 percent of lithium was mined in only three countries: Australia, Chile, and China. Six out of the ten largest lithium mines in the world were located in Australia.[1] However, the year of Putin's all-out war on Ukraine has also been the year of new permits for lithium exploration issued in Spain, Portugal, and the Czech Republic, among other countries. Preexisting environmental opposition from activist and civil society groups has been brushed off using the staple Republican discourse of "energy independence" prevalent in the United States since at least the 1980s and currently adapted to the harsh realities of Russia's unreliability as the main energy provider for the EU.

But what does the return of the repressed mean, particularly on the scale of world politics and taken in its full historical sense? Is this return a mere repetition of what happened in the past, or do unconscious mutations in the repressed content add something to each of its resurfacings?

Sigmund Freud coined the term "the return of the repressed" quite early in his career, in an 1896 letter to Wilhelm Fliess, and he stuck to it for the rest his life. According to Freud, this phenomenon is a part of "neuroses of repression," where psychic defenses ultimately fail, giving rise to a stage "in which the repressed ideas return, and in which, during the struggle between them and the ego, new symptoms are formed which are those of the illness proper."[2] Upon registering his insight into the return of the repressed, Freud accorded to it tremendous significance: he thought that "the main differences between the various neuroses are shown in the way in which the repressed ideas return" (*SE*, 1:223). The *how* of the return is thus reflective of obsessional, paranoiac, and hysterical types of neuroses.

In the early formulations of the return of the repressed, there is always a trigger event, "a contemporary psychical force" bringing with it "every fresh wave of the return" (*SE*, 1:225). And, regardless of the type of neurosis, these "waves" threaten with "overwhelming" of the ego (*SE*, 1:228), the collapse of the defensive barriers it had erected between itself and unacceptable unconscious content. When Freud circled back to the return of the repressed in the last years of his life, notably in his *Moses and Monotheism*, composed between 1934 and 1938 (that is, right before the start of World War II), he specified that the distinguishing mark of symptoms it provokes is "the far-reaching distortion to which the returning material has been subjected as compared to the original" (*SE*, 23:127). Curiously enough, he links this idea to a "historical truth" that is inseparable from a "delusion." "When Moses brought the people the idea of a single god," Freud writes, "it was not a novelty but signified the revival of an experience in the primaeval ages of the human family, which had long vanished from men's conscious memory.... An idea such as this has a compulsive character: it *must* be believed. To the extent to which it is distorted, it may be describe as *delusion*; in so far as it brings a return of the past, it must be called *truth*" (*SE*, 23:129–30).

Now we are ready to go back to the European context in 2022. Not by chance, war and mining are the repressed of contemporary politics and economy. What is repressed in and through them, as exceedingly *dirty affairs*, is the energy that, channeling raw libidinal forces, is entwined with large-scale destruction and, in the last instance, with the death drive. Pushed to the unconscious in a move that is geographically expressed in the relegation of both activities to other parts of the world, war and mining nonetheless persist, sustaining the presumably violence-free edifice of European politics. Parliamentary discussions and electoral debates (increasingly meaningless, because drained of the libidinal forces that had been originally bound in them), as well as the "clean energy" transition much vaunted at the highest levels of government and corporate structures, are the temporary substitutes for the geographically and psychically displaced military and mining ventures. As with all unconscious processes, though, displacement, creating "a *substitutive formation*" (*SE*, 14:154), is successful only up to a certain point: the repressed returns, precisely, when its chthonic, subterranean pressure breaks through the wall of defenses (or anti-cathexes) meant to keep it out of conscious grasp.

Without denying the genocidal conduct of the Russian army in Ukraine, if "Putin" is treated as a personification of pure evil in Europe today, that is because "he" is a symptom that no longer manages to keep what has been displaced and substituted under wraps—a face or a mask affixed to the European repressed as such. In the current historical conjuncture, then, we are living through the consequences of the return of the repressed as Freud has described them: the "struggle" between, on the one hand, repressed ideas concretized in war and mining and, on the other hand, the conscious ego (national and EU institutions), in the course of which "new symptoms are formed which are those of the illness proper." These "new symptoms" are the presumably reactive embrace of mining inside the EU and the exponential increase of military budgets, along with NATO expansion in Northern Europe, leading us to "the illness proper": the lack of deep changes in the European model of political and economic energy, of the extractive-destructive paradigm that is of a piece with capitalism.

Along similar lines, multiculturalism and the more recent turn to animism in progressive European circles do not signal a radical departure from "the idea of a single god" that, in Freud's analysis, is the Egyptian repressed returning in Mosaic religion and the Jewish repressed returning in Christianity.[3] Of course, repressed materials return "with a far-reaching distortion," which is itself double: the One is twisted into an illusion of multiplicity, while a religious artifact mutates into a secular idol, namely capital. Capitalist exchange value is not only abstract, as David Ricardo, Adam Smith, and Karl Marx acknowledged; it is extractive and destructive over and above the mining and wars that are necessary for "primitive accumulation," capital's incessantly repeated inaugural moment. In other words, capitalist abstraction is only possible by virtue of the prior and ongoing operations of extraction and destruction. As the kernel of what truly matters from the standpoint of capital, exchange value is extracted from commodities, including commodified labor, at the price of use value, the material body of the commodity, discarded as a useless shell. Mining is the literalization of this metaphysical movement; war is the concretization of its violent outcomes.

It may seem like a bit of a stretch to extend the strictly psychological return of the repressed to historical developments, but Freud himself highlights and validates this extension in his late work *Moses and Monotheism*. Here, as we have already seen, (historical) reality and (historical) delusion merge at the confluence of the "return" and the "repressed": for Freud, the repetition of the past constitutes historical truth, and the reemergence of qualitatively changed repressed contents in the course of repetition builds up a delusion regarding the novelty of what is taking place. Though the psychoanalytic historical scheme is already quite complicated, we cannot help but ask: Are things as simple as this? Does history unfold through the circularity of repetition, which is camouflaged as something new, because the repressed that returns at each one of its loops remains unrecognizable? Or is the dynamic *form* of repetition transfigured together with the distorted *content* of the repressed?

To begin answering these questions, we need to develop what I have called in my 2021 book *Senses of Upheaval* "a robust philosophy of history" capable of registering and thinking through historical "gaps, protracted subterranean processes, and time lags between causes and effects."[4] In this sense, it should be noted that the war in Ukraine is, in part, an outcome of time lags between the official end of the USSR in 1991 and its unresolved legacies, also responsible, following the example of the collapse of Yugoslavia, for the simmering conflict between Armenia and Azerbaijan in the Nagorno-Karabakh region or the tragic fate of Belarus. And constantly looming in the background is the issue of atomic energy, the distribution of the Soviet nuclear arsenal, and Russia's threats to deploy nonconventional weapons should the conflict either widen or deepen.

At the same time, the knots (cathexes and anti-cathexes) tied or untied in Putin's war in Ukraine involve much more than the as yet indeterminate legacy of Soviet collapse. To European observers, the war in Ukraine is redolent of the actions of Nazi Germany in 1939. To the Ukrainians themselves, it invariably brings to mind the national catastrophes of the recent past, from the 1932–33 Holodomor to enormous population losses suffered in World War II and the nightmare of the 1986 Chernobyl disaster. To the Russians who oppose the regime, the tightening of censorship and other internal repressive measures undertaken in the aftermath of the invasion awaken the memory of Stalinism. The amassing of repressed materials in one historical event implies that there is not a single History (mirroring the idea of the one God of monotheism, discussed by Freud). Instead, various histories intersect at this point, their effects both clashing and mutually reinforcing. In Freudian terms, the phenomenon is that of condensation, "appropriat[ing] the whole cathexis of several other ideas" that float in the unconscious (*SE*, 14:186) and channeling its energy into a single process or object.

The tired adage "history repeats itself," in which Freud saw the truth of history, no longer applies. Repetition entails cyclicality and definite temporal rhythms, not to mention the completion of whatever is being repeated. Yet, many of the issues at play in the current war and in mining are comet tails and incomplete events or ideas put into practice, from the dissolution of the Soviet Union to the effects of radioactive fallout that take thousands of years to wear off, from the still predominant extractive-destructive energy paradigm to firmly engrained totalitarian mindsets. So, what is happening if not a repetition of history?

I would like to suggest that history implodes, tumbling into itself in a vortex of events that give off an appearance of repetition. One indication concerning the implosion of history is the convergence of different timelines in the current war in Ukraine: the timeline of Soviet collapse thirty years ago, that of the Chernobyl disaster, which happened thirty-six years ago and unfurls an indefinite future of environmental contamination, that of the two World Wars, of the Ukrainian genocide and Stalinist repressions of the 1930s, and so on.

All this is concentrated in the current war, much as "fissionable material is compressed by powerful chemical explosives distributed over its external surface" in an implosion-type atomic bomb. "Because the explosives compress the core of the bomb, the implosion concept also yields a more efficient bomb—that is to say, one that produces the same amount of energy with a smaller mass of fissionable material."[5] The explosion of hostilities is, at its core, a historical implosion.

Although Freud did not venture beyond the repetition of history and its distorted forms, the psychoanalytic notion of condensation helps us understand history's implosion.

In dreams, condensation produces specific dream images by means of composite structures, gathered from many corners of the unconscious. "Dream-condensation" is the "uniting [of] the actual features of two or more people into a single dream-image" (*SE*, 4:293). The spatiotemporal convergence of different past disasters and their effects in Putin's war in Ukraine exemplifies a similar composite arrangement on a historical scale. The equivalent of a historical dream image of the victim includes elements of the Holodomor and Soviet collectivization, of Nazi genocide and those who suffered the effects of technogenic catastrophes (let's say, the effects of "mining the atom"), et cetera. The dream image of the aggressor is also a collage harking back to fragments of these events.

Within the apparatus of repression, the immense power of condensation is due to the fact that the "process of *condensation* has drawn the whole cathexis onto itself" (*SE*, 14:156). The concentrated charge of psychic energy it carries is explicable with reference to its function as a wholesale substitute for the forbidden affect. It is exceptionally close to the dangerous end goal of desire: the annihilation of the other, the assimilation of alterity, the appropriation of energy

as such and as a whole, or, in a word, everything
that the death drive signifies. Again, war and
mining (and—why not?—the one *as* the other:
mining *as* war on mountainous ecosystems, war
as mining the resources and human potential of
the country it is waged against) bespeak condensation projected onto history from the sphere of
psychical processes *proper*.

Finally, the mechanisms of displacement and
condensation are activated in the id in general,
where "there is nothing … that corresponds to the
idea of time" and where "the energy of instinctual
impulses is in a state different from that in the
other regions of the mind, far more mobile and
capable of discharge" (*SE*, 22:74–75). Rather than
the culmination of a succession, condensation in
the id heaps up disparate timelines and time scales
and gives off the impression of their instantaneous
accumulation in an extra-temporal present. The
volatility of the impulses it contains does not allow
this heap to provide any sort of support for the rest
of psychical life, nor, more importantly, any sense
of internal consistency or articulation among the
heaped-up materials: as the construction implodes,
pent-up energy explodes. That is why, when the
dams of anti-cathexis are breached, the repressed
does not return in a paced repetition but makes
itself felt with a bang, destroying the structures
built upon it, as on an active volcano.[6]

In turn, the three classical models that explain
the movement of history have included the conservative Fall, bemoaning the loss of past greatness;
liberal Progress, celebrating the opposite upward
vector of ever-improving life conditions and
ever-expanding markets; and cyclical repetition
(sometimes combined with the first or the second
model in a spiral) of world destruction and reju-
venation "by fire and water," as in Plato's *Timaeus*
(22c). None of these models, however, accounts for
unconscious depth, for multiple histories, and for

the kind of incompletion that exceeds the infinity
of a straight line or a circle. Each presupposes
a coherent, orderly unfolding in keeping with
the temporality of conscious life, with limited
applications to individual human beings, let alone
to groups and societies.

Implosion is the fourth option that similarly
borrows from physics (and from psychoanalysis)
to describe how "history" caves in under the mass
of unresolved legacies of heterogeneous events
and processes. An inward collapse then coincides
with a series of pyropolitical explosions.[7] In a way,
the fourth model combines elements from the
other three, pitting conservative against liberal
visions and exhibiting aspects of repetition as a
consequence of the centripetal forces unleashed
in an implosion. This is why we hear echoes of "the
restoration" of the glorious past of the Russian
Empire, of the "irrepressible" march toward
market freedom and democracy in Ukraine, and,
last but not least, of the tirelessly repeated mantra
"history repeats itself."

The implosion of history is equally palpable
in the global environmental crisis, where the event
of the sixth mass extinction that is underway
is not merely a repetition of the previous five
mass extinctions but also the collapse of human
species-history, among the histories of countless
other species. In the geological epoch of the
Anthropocene, this collapse is self-provoked, as
far as agriculture and the Industrial Revolution
are concerned, and, therefore, bears all the
marks of an implosion within the framework
of the natural-cultural history of *Homo sapiens*.
The centrality of fossil fuels to environmental
degradation and to the possibilities of funding
Putin's regime holds a clue to their cobelonging
within the paradigm of the implosion of history:
to reiterate, mining and war are two facets of the
same return of the repressed in Europe today.

Here President Volodymyr Zelenskyy emerges as a new Greta Thunberg–like figure vis-à-vis the West, "speaking truth to power" and eliciting standing ovations from parliaments around the world, but to no avail.

The perennial question of political action—"what is to be done?"—cannot be raised seriously without at least a rough understanding of the historical situation in which such an action hopes to be effective. Is the persistence of mining in the current "energy transition" a not-so-subtle reminder about the staying power of the extractive-destructive energy paradigm? Is anything like a transition even possible if our energy dreams and desires are governed by the forces of the id, which has nothing "that corresponds to the idea of time"? Is the war in Ukraine a provisional setback on the road to freedom, spreading around the world? Is it a temporary obstacle to the atavistic, colonial restoration of Russia's imperial greatness, in line with the equally atavistic dependence on fossil fuels? Does it repeat World War II in reverse, with the defenders of their homeland now in the position of occupiers?

One characteristic of the implosion of history is that it draws everything and everyone into its vortex. If, indeed, the war in Ukraine is a telltale sign of the implosion, then it is naive to think that, though it is still early to talk about World War III, the hostilities taking place on Ukrainian soil are limited to the territory on which they are unfolding. The imbrication of nuclear issues in the conflict, including nuclear power plants and atomic weapons, is symptomatic of the temporally and spatially unlimited effects of these hostilities. Widespread questioning of the efficacy of international institutions, including the UN, or of the previously nonaligned position of some countries (Finland, Sweden) means that Russia's invasion of Ukraine has shaken the foundations of the current

73

world order. Closely interrelated global food and energy crises aggravated, albeit not really caused, by the war add fuel to the fire of the implosion.

In their volatility, the instinctual impulses released in the implosion of history recognize neither temporal nor spatial boundaries: in psychoanalytic terms, the implosion points toward the possibility of a psychotic breakdown, rather than toward neurotic symptom formation, circumscribed by the walls of repression or anti-cathexes. After condensation "has drawn the whole cathexis into itself," it spews outward what it has drawn in, combining an implosion with a powerful explosion. The sooner this logic (or illogic) is grasped, the better we will be able to respond to the urgent question, "What is to be done?" For we are living not only at the end of an era with an acute sense of the end of history, but also, and more significantly, at the end of how we see history itself.

1 "World's Ten Largest Lithium
   Mines in the World in 2020,"
   Mining Technology, September
   8, 2021, https://www.mining-
   technology.com/marketdata/ten-
   largest-lithiums-mines-2020-2/,
   accessed October 27, 2022.
2 *The Standard Edition of the
   Complete Psychological Works
   of Sigmund Freud*, trans. and ed.
   James Strachey, 24 vols. (London:
   Vintage, 2001), vol. 1, p. 222
   (hereafter cited in the text as *SE*).
3 As an echo of Freud's "Moses,
   the Egyptian," we could say
   today, "Putin, the German."
4 Michael Marder, *Senses
   of Upheaval: Philosophical
   Snapshots of a Decade* (London:
   Anthem, 2021), pp. 11–12.
5 Georges Charpak and Richard
   L. Garwin, *Megawatts and
   Megatons: The Future of
   Nuclear Power and Nuclear
   Weapons* (Chicago: University
   of Chicago Press, 2002), p. 60.
6 Note that the composite
   aquatic, fiery, and artifact-based
   dream image of the "heap" that
   emerges here reflects the logic
   of unconscious condensation.
7 For more on such explosions,
   consult Michael Marder,
   *Pyropolitics: When the World
   Is Ablaze* (London: Rowman
   & Littlefield, 2015).

Fears and Prejudices

Martin Pollack

77

Russia's war of aggression against Ukraine has shaken Europe to its very foundations. Old fears and prejudices that we thought we had overcome long ago are once again surfacing. Now we are forced to realize that we had merely blocked and repressed them, because that was easier than dealing with their root causes. Although looking back may be painful, it can help us to understand at least some of what we are facing today.

A trip I took long ago to Prague, in 1960, comes to mind. I took a train from Linz to České Budějovice, Budweis, where I changed trains for Prague. On the train to Prague, a young woman in uniform, plump, blond, and pretty, was checking tickets. I don't remember there being any women in that position in Austria at the time.

The train was empty, so she sat down next to me. She spoke only a few words of German and I spoke no Czech, but we had a wonderful conversation nonetheless. We laughed and bantered, and I gave her some bananas and a pack of cigarettes I had picked up at the request of an acquaintance for a friend in Prague. The cigarettes, sold in tin boxes of twenty-five each, bore the foreign-sounding name "Khedive." The boxes were adorned with colorful pictures from the Orient, showing a white city with minarets and a portrait of a mustachioed Arab with a fluttering headdress, who seemed to attract particular interest from my new acquaintance. In thanks, she gave me a kiss on the cheek.

I had pictured communism differently, somehow stricter.

I felt really special. Like a messenger from another, better world who generously came bearing gifts to this country where everything from the West was admired, earning shining eyes and gratitude in return. It was only years later that it dawned on me that I had behaved like a miniature colonial overlord pretending to be a benefactor.

This paternalistic attitude toward Eastern
Europe, which we once so sweepingly and disdain-
fully dubbed the Eastern Bloc, has persisted in the
West for decades, often to this day, even after the
so-called Eastern Bloc has long since disappeared.
This arrogant viewpoint was accompanied by
the conviction that the people over there, behind
the Iron Curtain, had only themselves to blame
for their plight, because they were indolent and
unwilling to improve their situation on their own
initiative. That they were victims of a history over
which they had little influence was something we
were reluctant to acknowledge.

We thus came to develop a feeling of superiority toward our poor neighbors who were deprived
of their freedom, a feeling that was coupled with
the kind of contempt that travelers often show
to natives in distant lands whom they deem to
be on a lower rung of civilization, comparable to
helpless children.

We tend to ignore here the extent to which
our relations with the countries in the East are in
fact historically fraught. Germans and Austrians
wreaked more havoc in these areas during the 20th
century than hardly anywhere else. In no other part
of Europe were entire populations so systematically
and brutally uprooted and shunted back and forth,
from East to West and back again. Expulsions,
deportations, and so-called purges to which tens of
thousands fell victim were the order of the day.

The fact that our fathers and grandfathers were
among the perpetrators responsible for the worst
crimes, chief among them the Holocaust, was for a
long time either concealed or denied. In Austria, a
collective amnesia set in after 1945 that left a deep
imprint. The country became an inglorious example
of the sloppy handling of the past, its attitude
characterized by both complacency and repression.
No one wanted to admit to having known about
the outrages committed, not even the perpetrators

themselves. Germany undertook much greater
efforts to come to terms with its past, and yet there,
too, widespread forgetting soon set in.

Shortly after a catastrophe that went beyond
anything ever seen before, we quickly accustomed
ourselves again to living in a seemingly idyllic,
safe world, without feeling any guilt. This complacency was made possible by a willingness to lay a
cloak of silence over the dark secrets of the past.
Anyone who violated this tacit commandment,
one that was not officially decreed but nevertheless universally welcomed, was vilified as an
annoying troublemaker.

This attitude was made all the easier when the
countries most haunted by the past disappeared
behind the Iron Curtain after the end of the war. In
the first postwar years, that boundary line posed
an almost insurmountable bulwark that aroused
both dull fears and denial. All of a sudden, regions
that only yesterday had seemed so close by and
familiar took on a remote air, like lands that were
utterly different and inaccessible.

One consequence of this development was
a keen feeling of alienation between people in
the East and West, one that still persists today. It
took a long time until we finally started to make
an effort to bridge the deep divide. And yet today
we increasingly find ourselves wondering whether
we have succeeded at all. Is it not the case instead
that the former antagonisms are still simmering
beneath the surface, having merely been glossed
over for a brief time?

I know it is not considered elegant to quote
oneself, but I will make an exception here. In
2005, in the preface to a volume of essays I edited
titled *Sarmatische Landschaften: Nachrichten
aus Litauen, Beloruss, der Ukraine, Polen und
Deutschland* (Sarmatian Landscapes: News
from Lithuania, Belarus, Ukraine, Poland, and
Germany), I wrote: "Ignorance, lack of awareness,

and disinterest in anything one might superficially call 'the East,' coupled with a healthy dose of fear and mistrust—this mix has perennially provided the mortar for building walls behind which people defined themselves in distinction from the others, those over there, those from the East."[1]

Of course, much has changed since then; borders have disappeared or at least become more permeable, and conflicts have been settled, but in many cases these changes were only superficial, as it now turns out. Too much optimism would arguably be misplaced. We might sometimes get the impression instead that it is an almost hopeless endeavor to try to finally overcome old prejudices and clichés regarding the others, whom we regard as strangers, and often as enemies.

It would seem to me that an indispensable prerequisite for getting past these entrenched viewpoints would be an active willingness to dispel prevailing ignorance regarding, for example, the countries in eastern Central Europe, to avoid the frequently misused term Eastern Europe. The latest political developments, including burgeoning autocratic tendencies that have culminated in the establishment of blatant dictatorships in Russia and Belarus, along with the rise of right-wing nationalist, authoritarian currents and parties in countries with what were once considered consolidated democracies, are posing serious obstacles to this path. We have only ourselves to blame for having been lulled into a false sense of security for so long, much too long, and for having shut our eyes to reality. A bitter revenge is now looming.

One example of this denial of reality is the incredulity and surprise with which most people in free Europe, including and especially politicians, have reacted to Russia's war of aggression. For many, Ukraine remained a terra incognita, even after proclaiming its independence in 1991. It was a country about which we knew hardly anything and, let's be honest, one that interested us little. Does it even exist as an independent country with its own history, culture, and language? Some of these knowledge gaps have been filled in recent years, at least in the literary realm. Authors such as Serhiy Zhadan, Andrey Kurkov, and Yuri Andrukhovych, to name but a few, are enjoying growing popularity in the German-speaking world—and yet on the whole Ukraine still seems like a foreign world. This is even truer for other countries such as Belarus, a state that has not been able to break away from Russia's sphere of influence, or the Republic of Moldova.

It is a tragic irony of fate that these countries only obtrude on our consciousness when they are stricken by severe crises or even wars. This has also been the fate of Ukraine. Vladimir Putin's war of aggression, in violation of all international laws and treaties, has in one fell swoop brought Ukraine to the attention of the world. People stare spellbound at images of a war that is devastating large swaths of the country, laying waste to towns and villages, and costing so many lives, those of soldiers and civilians alike. Putin has bluntly declared his determination to destroy the country and, with it, all those who insist on the independence of Ukraine, regardless of the consequences for both his own country and Ukraine. Alongside the military battle, he is waging no less doggedly and infamously an unprecedented information war against the country.

Putin denies Ukraine any right to an independent status, claiming that the country does not even exist on its own, that it never existed, that the Ukrainian territories have always been part of the Russian Empire and must now be brought back into the fold of the Greater Russian Empire that he promises to establish. He has set out to consistently eradicate the national identity of Ukraine, an identity he categorically denies. This is not a notion invented by Putin but rather a goal that is deeply rooted in the history of Great Russian imperialism, one that already motivated the actions of the tsars. That this view is now also being entertained by many people in the West indicates an alarming breakdown within Europe.

The war Putin has unleashed, which may not even be called by that name in Russia, did not begin in February of this year but in fact much earlier: in 2014, when Putin annexed Crimea and supported the separatists in Donbas not only with propaganda but with weapons and troops in their efforts to secede from Ukraine and become part of Russia. From Putin's imperialist and revisionist point of view, his approach seems only logical—he had articulated these same intentions before, if we had only paid close enough attention to what he said and wrote.

As early as 2005, Putin described in a much-publicized speech the disintegration of the Soviet Union as "the greatest geopolitical catastrophe of the [20th] century," suggesting his objective to restore and consolidate a totalitarian order in Russia—under his leadership, of course. Step by step, he eliminated all opposition on his path to unchallenged autocracy, in the process declaring freedom of expression, indeed freedom as a whole, to be the enemy. To secure his power, the former intelligence officer did not shy away from applying the most drastic methods, up to and including murder. A new, all-powerful, and infallible tsar was born.

"Self-heroization and messiahship result in a feeling of responsibility not to the people but to history," noted Russian political scientist Tatiana Stanovaya in her analysis of Putin's boundless claim to power, published in the Russian online magazine Republic in July 2021.[2] To German ears, this is bound to sound familiar. Putin knows that he can only achieve his most ardent goal, the reestablishment of a Greater Russian Empire,

if he succeeds in conquering the territories of
Ukraine—home of the Kievan Rus' state to which
today's Russia traces its origins—thus robbing
them of their independence.

And that means war. This is a war that many
here in Austria initially regarded as none of our
business, because it was being waged elsewhere,
in a world that seemed completely alien to us. We
look on and register with horror the appalling
images of the victims and the mass destruction.
Only the fact that the war appears to be so far
away is able to reassure us to some extent. But is
the war really so distant? Isn't that notion mere
wishful thinking that turns a blind eye to reality?
After all, the former Austrian city of Lemberg, Lviv,
now being shelled and bombed by the Russians,
is closer to Vienna than Bregenz is. What's more,
far-sighted observers are slowly coming to the
realization that the war is directed not only against
Ukraine but against the whole of free Europe.
Nevertheless, more and more voices in our countries are calling on Ukraine to seek dialogue with
the aggressor and to commence negotiations.

Many people in free Europe have contentedly
settled into ignorance and let themselves be
swayed by Russian propaganda. Foreignness and
distance can seem threatening, but sometimes they
also have something reassuring about them, for
example when it comes to war. The further away,
the better. This thinking may not be compatible
with solidarity, but it is certainly convenient. It was
an Austrian author who advised the Ukrainians to
surrender immediately to avoid further bloodshed.
Better a coward than dead.

Other Austrian and German intellectuals do
not go quite that far, but they, too, feel called upon
to urge from a safe distance that Ukraine should
seek negotiations with the invader, even if it means
making compromises, which, given Putin's brutal
resolve, would inevitably involve ceding territory

and even the loss of national independence. Can we really ask this of the Ukrainians, who have only just won their independence, in good conscience? I hardly think so.

History never repeats itself exactly, and yet it would seem legitimate at this point to recall Adolf Hitler's efforts to impose his will on one country after another until he plunged all of Europe into war. Then as now, many initially believed that the aggressor had to be accommodated, if necessary by making generous compromises at the expense of those who were weaker. Appeasement was the order of the day, and we all know where that led.

To repeat: the war that is intended to help Putin lead Russia to new greatness is only at first glance being waged against Ukraine alone. The truth is that it is really about democracy, about freedom, about the whole of free Europe, even if many do not want to admit this because they prefer to close their eyes to the facts, just as so many politicians and business leaders have done in the past. They don't like to be reminded of that today. We only ever had the good of the country and the economy in mind, they say now.

It is not easy to accept that so many decision-makers until only recently put their faith in a ruthless dictator like Putin, hanging on his every word. That they willingly swallowed his lies, even though he made little effort to hide his true intentions. Is this a matter of simple naivety, of ignorance, of a refusal to acknowledge reality, or perhaps more a case of sheer greed? Experience shows that good deals can be made with dictators. This insight is not new. We can still remember how Swiss banks unquestioningly bought up Nazi gold while the Nazis were robbing and murdering Jews in the countries they occupied. It took a long time for these shameful dealings to come to light. Forgetting and repression accompany the history of all wars.

Conveniently, the mass murders during World War II took place in far-off regions, in occupied Poland, Belarus, the Baltic countries, and the territories of today's Ukraine. And there we have it again, this distance and foreignness that seem almost comfortable to us, evidently making it so easy to ignore the most horrific of events. Often, in open contradiction to the facts, there is also a kind of reversal of perpetrator and victim, or the two are at least put on equal footing.

What about the question of guilt? Is it even legitimate to ask that question? The past has taught us that this is a dangerous minefield. And yet it seems essential that we state the circumstances clearly. In a recent interview with the American historian and Ukraine expert Marci Shore, Ukrainian writer Volodymyr Rafeyenko, referring to the refusal of many Western observers to acknowledge Russia's sole culpability in the war, said: "It's no longer possible to bury your head in the sand and not see. If you *do not* see the Russian atrocities, if you do not see Russia as an anthropological catastrophe, you are consciously not seeing it. In this way, you are also making a choice between good and evil."[3]

Of course, there are often reasons that are difficult to grasp at first glance for hesitating to condemn an attacker unequivocally from the outset or to support the attacked without reservation. These reasons are usually to be found in history. To stay with the example of Ukraine: many try to explain Germany's dithering attitude toward the maltreated nation of Ukraine by citing its guilt complex with regard to Russia in view of the terrorism perpetrated there by Nazi Germany, which claimed millions of Russian victims, soldiers as well as civilians.

This guilt complex may seem justified, because World War II did exact an extraordinarily bloody toll on Russia, more so than on other countries.

However, this attitude fails to acknowledge the fact (which is deliberately denied by Russia) that it was precisely the territories of today's Ukraine, in other words ethnic Ukrainians, who bore the brunt of the German atrocities. The acts of war covered the entire Ukrainian terrain and made Ukrainians victims, while the vast reaches of Russia were less affected simply because of geographical conditions. Ethnic Ukrainians were also represented disproportionately among the soldiers of the Red Army.

Without by any means wanting to downplay the Russian victims, it must be kept in mind that the official Russian narrative, elevated to the status of sacred truth in times of war, according to which the Russians fought heroically in the "Great Patriotic War" and suffered the most casualties, while the majority of Ukrainians collaborated with Hitler, does not stand up to historical scrutiny. The official Russian account that the invasion of Ukraine was unavoidable because the country supposedly needs to be "denazified," whatever that means, doesn't help either.

In the West, the Ukrainian victims of World War II were and still are often overlooked because many people continue to perceive the country as a foreign body in Europe with which they have no connection. When speaking of the victims in this region, one usually referred to Soviet citizens, who were equated with ethnic Russians. Such simplifications have a long tradition. When I began to study in Poland in the 1960s, the countless memorial plaques and monuments to the victims of World War II showed only that Polish citizens had been murdered there, even if the victims were Jewish. They were not mentioned specifically, or rather, they were not allowed to be mentioned. It was similar elsewhere. People who belong to minorities usually go unnamed as victims of war; they disappear amid the majority population, as if

it were not worth citing them specifically. In many
cases, this was and even still is explicitly prohibited.

It is a feature of our times that history is
now being rewritten in many places. This is
done entirely according to the demands and the
discretion of the respective rulers, who regard
history as a welcome tool for legitimizing their
claim to power and suppressing other opinions.
That is also the case in Russia, where Putin has
elevated himself to the position of supreme
history teacher, not least in order to enforce his
unalterable conviction that Ukraine historically
belongs to Russia and has no right to an independent existence. Another claim, raised by the
official historiography to the status of universal
truth, is that the Russians have always been either
heroes or victims, never incurring the weight of
historical guilt.

This instrumentalization of history, which
brooks no contradictions, can also be found elsewhere, for example in Poland. There, as in Russia,
the powers that be are using all the means at their
disposal to establish the thesis that Poles have historically always and without exception been either
heroes or victims but never perpetrators. It is not
only Jewish-Polish historians who vehemently
contradict this assertion by continually presenting
new evidence that many Poles participated in the
extermination of Jews during World War II (and in
the period immediately thereafter).

Historical wounds have thus never been given
a chance to heal; on the contrary, they continually
threaten to be reopened at every suitable occasion,
leading to bloody confrontations. In order to avoid
this eventuality, it is imperative that we relentlessly
investigate and lay bare the crimes and outrages
of the past in order to reach an understanding
with the descendants of the former victims. In my
opinion, there is no other option. Concealment
and suppression are not a viable way out.

The Balkan wars in the 1990s after the
break-up of Yugoslavia are a convincing example
of this fact. For decades, the conflicts between the
nations and ethnic groups in the multiethnic state
had been covered in a cloak of silence at Josip Broz
Tito's command and, if necessary, suppressed with
an iron hand. The consequences are well known:
an outbreak of internecine hatred that resulted in
unimaginable atrocities.

Russia could face a similar fate, because Putin
adamantly refuses to countenance a critical examination of his country's history. On the contrary,
official historiography casts that history in a halo
of glory—any confession of guilt, whether toward
other peoples or one's own population, is a closely
guarded taboo. There was a time when things were
different, but Putin has now turned back the clock.
Joseph Stalin's crimes, for example, are once
more being denied or at least covered up, first and
foremost the Holodomor, the famine in Ukraine
in the 1930s, which Stalin deliberately induced and
which cost the lives of millions of Ukrainians. The
same applies to the crimes being committed in the
current war, the countless murders of civilians, the
rapes, and looting.

This year's winner of the Peace Prize of the
German Book Trade, Serhiy Zhadan, said in a
recent interview that a dialogue between Ukraine
and Russia is unthinkable "as long as Russian
society does not take collective responsibility for
everything they did in Ukraine."[4]

We know from experience how difficult it is
for governments to distance themselves from past
deeds and to accept something like collective
responsibility for them. In Austria, it took decades
for a chancellor to finally apologize for involvement in the Holocaust during a visit to Israel.

The renowned Ukrainian historian Andrii
Portnov has said that Russia needs a "culture of
guilt," which means that those responsible must

deal openly and in an unvarnished manner with
the crimes of the past and present. Of course, this
also applies to the severely damaged, perhaps
irreparable, relations between Russia and
Ukraine. Portnov quoted the words of the Russian
philologist Mikhail Gasparov, who died in 2005:
"We (Russians) must atone (to Ukraine), this is our
moral duty; if every enlightened Russian does not
feel (this guilt), it is bitter and strange."[5]
    Whether this realization will ever prevail in
Putin's Russia seems doubtful. And yet we know
from our own experience that there is no way
around it. It does not help in such cases to look
away and shrug our shoulders while refusing to take
action. We have to admit to ourselves that it was
our own courting of Putin, our shameless efforts
to curry favor with him, that made him what he is
today. Banks, industrialists, and politicians had only
their own profit in mind. Demonstrating both a lack
of scruples and obstinate stupidity, they ignored
the dangers lurking in their dealings—dangers that
have now been tragically confirmed. *Après moi, le
deluge.* Today we, and above all the Ukrainians, are
paying for this blindness.
    History teaches us that we must not hesitate
to condemn the aggressor and to show solidarity
with and aid those under attack. Otherwise, we
make ourselves complicit and end up becoming
victims ourselves.

August 2022

Translated from the German by Jennifer Taylor

1   Martin Pollack, introduction to
    *Sarmatische Landschaften:
    Nachrichten aus Litauen,
    Beloruss, der Ukraine, Polen und
    Deutschland*, ed. Martin Pollack
    (Frankfurt am Main: S. Fischer,
    2005). Unless otherwise noted, all
    translations are by Jennifer Taylor.

2   Tatiana Stanovaya, "Politicheskii
    bespilotnik, ili Pochemu Kremliu
    bol´she ne nuzhna legitimnost´,"
    Republic, July 26, 2021, republic.
    ru/posts/101129; "Alles auf
    Autopilot," trans. Hartmut
    Schröder, Dekoder, August 12,
    2021, https://www.dekoder.
    org/de/article/stanowaja-
    analyse-legimitaet-dumawahl,
    accessed November 14, 2022.

3   Volodymyr Rafeyenko, "Writing
    Off Russia," interview by Marci
    Shore, Project Syndicate,
    July 1, 2022, https://www.
    project-syndicate.org/onpoint/
    ukraine-war-impact-on-russian-
    writer-by-volodymyr-rafeyenko-
    and-marci-shore-2022-06,
    accessed November 3, 2022.

4   Quoted in Andrii Portnov,
    "Russland braucht eine
    Schuldkultur," *Neue Zürcher
    Zeitung*, July 20, 2022, https://
    www.nzz.ch/feuilleton/
    russland-braucht-eine-
    schuldkultur-ld.1693068,
    accessed November 3, 2022.

5   Ibid.

The Fascism of Ambiguity

Marcia Sá Cavalcante Schuback

95

In an article in *The New York Times*, prominent historian Timothy Snyder recently affirmed the need to identify Russia's current regime as a fascist one. This serves to undermine the "undermining propaganda" used by Vladimir Putin's regime to justify Russia's war on Ukraine. To call someone a "fascist" or "Nazi" means invoking the memory of World War II and designating an enemy. The need to designate enemies with hate speech makes it easier to murder them. Putin speaks of the Ukrainians as fascists and Nazis, activating past hate speech against those fascists and Nazis who used hate speech in the past against the Russians. As Snyder observes, when we see and hear fascists calling other people "fascist," "hate speech inverts reality and propaganda to its illogical extreme as a cult of unreason." This new fascist practice of inverting every meaning to the extreme, in which anti-fascist and fascist discourses are inverted, confused, and reversible, Snyder calls "schizofascism," and Ukrainians found an even better term: "ruscism."[1]

I have tried to philosophically grasp this practice with the conceptual expression "fascism of ambiguity." There is a crucial need today to clarify this practice of rendering the term "fascism" ambiguous and to understand it as part of an effort to render every meaning ambiguous for the sake of undermining the practice of senses. In an eponymous book, written before the invasion of Ukraine and with Jair Bolsonaro and Donald Trump in mind, I have sketched out fundamental points of historical fascism in Italy as formulated by Benito Mussolini, Pier Paolo Pasolini's thoughts on the new form of fascism he observed growing after the war with mass society, and the need to define the new form of fascism in our contemporary age, anchored in a politics of the muddling of meanings.[2]

97

Fascism is, as we know, a term coined by Mussolini to designate the party he founded in January 1915, the Fascist Revolutionary Party. In the famous entry on fascism written by Mussolini and the philosopher Giovanni Gentile for the 1932 edition of the *Enciclopedia Italiana*, Mussolini insists that even in that first period his only doctrine was a "doctrine of action."[3] Denying the doctrine of socialism an effective practice, he declared the *practice* of socialist doctrine as the foundation of fascism. The goal was not a theory of action, but fascism as a "need to act" and fight, hence the name he conferred to the Fasci italiani di combattimento (Italian Fasces of Combat) movement.

As a doctrine of action, fascism claimed to be contrary to doctrinal expressions, asserting itself as a set of "aphorisms, anticipations and aspirations," a political doctrine that pretended to be completely different from all the previous ones. If this new style of writing a doctrine of action, intended by fascism, lacks carefully elaborated ideas or logically linked paragraphs, it replaces doctrine with words of "faith." *The aim was to appropriate the socialist desire for action.* Its intention was to touch the people without mediation, that is, to cause emotion, a verb that literally means to set the people in motion, without the mediation of the mechanisms of representation, understood by Mussolini and other political theorists of the time as the undemocratic stain of democracy. Fascism designated a doctrine of action whose objective was to implement a State of the people represented directly by the *duce*, a word that means "conductor."

Mussolini's entry in the *Enciclopedia* is revealing. It affirms a new style of doctrine: aphorismatic, anticipatory, aspiring, and "nondoctrinal." We thus find defined more of a change in the style of ideological language instead of a new ideology.

98

The ideological language gains a new aesthetic. This is an important first point to be kept in mind when trying to clarify the nebulosity of the concept of fascism today.

The second point to be highlighted is the difference that Mussolini makes between theoretical doctrine and doctrine of action and the pathos of mobilization of that doctrine, a mobilization that must be total, recalling the title of the famous essay by Ernst Jünger.[4] Fascism always says: no more theories, no more words; it is time not only to act, but also to act from beginning to end. In these formulations, fascism is a mobilizing and distorting appropriation of Karl Marx's eleventh thesis on Feuerbach: "Philosophers have hitherto only interpreted the world in various ways; the point is to change it."[5]

Fascism distorts because it does not want transformation but the deformation and extermination of the world. Indeed, it substitutes the senses of transformation with the powerful meaning of destruction. But how does this doctrine work? It acts bellicosely, repudiating all pacifist doctrine: "War alone keys up all human energies to their maximum tension and sets the seal of nobility on those peoples who have the courage to face it," as Mussolini states.[6] Fascist ultranationalism brings people together in an immediate relationship with the *duce*, their conductor, who is seen—coinciding with what is experienced—as their "direct representative," unmediated and, in this union, generating the electrifying experience of uncontrolled human energy.

The *duce*, the great conductor, is the electrifying conductor of all human energy that only in war—that is, in hatred—reaches its maximum tension. In the words of Mussolini, this anti-pacifist spirit inhabits not only the people, but each individual who, even though wounded in war, writes on their bandages *me ne frego* ("I don't give a

damn" or "so what?") to demonstrate not only
an "act of philosophic stoicism" or to "sum up
a doctrine which is not merely political," but
also to provide "evidence of a fighting spirit
which accepts all risks. It signifies a new style of
Italian life."[7] In the same passage, Mussolini also
speaks of how fascism is "love of life" conceived
as struggle, duty, and conquest, as a life lived for
oneself and above all as a life lived for others and
their substitutes. This love of life is "love of one's
neighbor," the entry continues, not the vague and
abstract neighbor of a "universal embrace," but
the differentiated neighbor watched with vigilant
eyes.[8] It is a life understood as the selective and
natural proximity of the strongest.

According to Mussolini, it is this conception of
life that opposes fascism to Marxist and scientific
socialism, and to the materialist conception of
history. He considers the latter to only aim at
the economic well-being of the people. But for
the fascism formulated in this entry, economic
well-being cannot be equated with happiness,
because the issue is "spiritual" well-being. In
addition to combating Marxist socialism, fascism
combats democratic ideology and its liberalism by
considering that it represents the "lie of political
equalitarianism, the habit of collective irrespon-
sibility," propagated by the "myth of felicity and
indefinite progress." If democracy is understood,
on the contrary, as "meaning a regime in which
the masses are not driven back to the margin of
the State," then fascism can be described as "an
organized, centralized, authoritarian democracy."[9]
Fascism presents itself, therefore, as a conception
of life practiced as a fight against Marxist socialism
and liberal democracy. It is an anti-pacifist life,
that is, an armed life, but at no point in the
entry does it "anticipate" what kind of life may
emerge after total mobilization, after total war. In
acclaiming war as the highest tension of all human

energy, fascism—this is hyperbolically valid for
Nazism—proclaims an absolutely final purpose, an
end without an after, the end as an end.

Living to die—no materialism can be more
immaterial than the fascist cult of the spirit.
Fascism is by definition necropolitics. Mass graves
are never some accident of fascist wars of destruction but an expected consequence of it. Fascism
is the experience of a bond around necropolitics,
the experience of the "common" mobilized by the
fascist doctrine of action and the "love of life in
death" that for me legitimize the use of the term
"fascism" and not "populism," "conservatism,"
or simply "authoritarianism" to designate the
mobilization of destructive forces—and not
"obscure"—operating today among us, with the
purpose of conducting (*ducere*) human energy to
the point of maximum tension.

In the 1960s, Pier Paolo Pasolini wrote a
lot about the new form of fascism that he saw
emerging in the postwar period. In his *Corsair
Writings*, his journalistic chronicles and essays,
there are inspiring visions for an attempt to think
about the ontological mutation through which the
new form of fascism could develop. According to
Pasolini, neofascism arises from within the new
form of capitalism closely allied to the new forms
of technology called, in his time, televisual technology and their resulting consolidation of society
and mass culture. With his kinetically critical eye,
he saw the new means of communication and
information operationalize and effect a "cultural
genocide," the extermination of values, souls,
language, gestures, and people's bodies.[10]

Through the senses, he sees an "anthropological
mutation" and "cultural indifferentiation" operated
upon senses, through which fascism is finally able
to effect a mutation of human consciousness and
sensitivity once every sense is replaced by "a potent
abstraction, [by] a pragmatism that cancerizes the

whole of society, a major central tumor..., a disease that contaminates the social fabric at all levels, an ideological disease that affects the soul and does not exempt any soul."[11]

Thus understood, neofascism represents a profound break with the forms of organization and discursive formulas of historical fascism because it comes from the transmuted background of human consciousness. The disappearance of "spirit" and "popular culture" and their replacement by media culture are for Pasolini ferocious testimonies of "cultural genocide" and "loss of linguistic ability" that characterize the "power of consumption." According to him, historical fascism, which he also calls "paleofascism," had never been fascist because it had failed to transmute the depth of the human soul, the mode of being human. That is why it was still possible to find forms of resistance to fascism. Only the power of consumption was able to achieve total fascism, the one that absorbs in its logic all forms of resistance and exposes fascism operating even within anti-fascism.[12] Still to explain and understand is how this absolutization proceeds.

Pasolini finds evidence of this "unpredictably new" form in an event. He saw through his "senses" that "something" had happened and that this "something" was the disappearance of fireflies in the Italian landscape.[13] In the poem "The Resistance and Its Light" and in a well-known text in which he speaks of "the disappearance of fireflies," Pasolini explains the political-existential vertigo of this event.[14] For him, fireflies are the flashing lights of resistance to the extermination of life within life, which broadly defines fascism. The poetic force of this image of resistance has inspired several discussions, especially in the quest to revive the sense of resistance in a world like ours, which is increasingly resistant to resistances.[15]

To discuss the issue of resistance fireflies, however, it is also necessary to understand how

the "power of consumption" is capable of fully
realizing neofascism, the total control of human
consciousness and sensibility. Pasolini refers to
the disappearance of fireflies as "the event of
something": "Something has happened." What
happened to make the fireflies disappear? I want to
propose that the mutation of every thing into "any
thing" and nothing, in effect, the mutation of every
thing into any thing is what happened. Pasolini's
discussions reveal not only an anthropological
but also an ontological mutation, a mutation of
the sense of being. By saying "something," Pasolini
touches the heart of neofascism, which is the
power of the emptiness of sense and meaning: the
emptying of the sense and meaning of people, of
gesture, of life, of human being, of existence, of
body, of soul, of politics, of society, of language,
the emptying of being and its senses, in short, the
emptying of the sense of sense. The "power of
consumption," by which a "cultural genocide" and
an "anthropological mutation" are carried out, is
the power of the emptiness and the indifference of
sense, a new sense of sense, the mutation of sense
itself. Pasolini does not develop the question of
the mutation of sense. He insists on the "loss of
linguistic ability."

By surprising the unpredictable "neofascist"
form of the power of consumption of a "televisual
neocapitalism," Pasolini clearly saw that "planetary
capitalism," no longer productive but financial
and monetary, is telemediatic capitalism. For him,
neofascism no longer needed any form or value
from historical fascism: tradition, family, or religion.
When pulling man from man, body from body, soul
from soul, the neofascism of consumer society and
mass culture realized what no ideological content
of the previous fascism had achieved: the lethal
mutation of human sensibility and consciousness.

But how, then, do we comprehend the reaction-
ism and pushback that accompanies what we are

calling fascism today? In a world where any-end-justifies-the-means is universalized, where absolute finality has no finality, how do we comprehend the moralizing and conservative discourse that circulates everywhere? Indeed, we must start from what, at first sight, constitutes a surprising contradiction that must be posed as a guiding question: How is it possible that technoplanetarian, neoliberal, financial capitalism, unthinkable without the new forms of information technology, robotics, algorithms, social media, media spectacle, and artificial intelligence, that is, capitalism without borders, essentially "internationalist"—because today power is entirely in the digital hands of inter-, multi-, and transnational conglomerates—lives so well alongside authoritarian, nationalist, protectionist, and patriotic governments?

These questions arise when we assume that, in order to understand the new form of fascism that is afflicting and plaguing our time, it is necessary to understand the new form of worldwide "capitalism" that causes it. It is impossible to conceive one without the other. Our starting point is that, from the point of view of its internal logic, neoliberal, technomediatic, and financial capitalism has fascism as its system and as its allied force. In its new form, fascism exposes how, in the age of planetary technique, man ceases to be the subject of history, as the new subject becomes technique: technoplanetarian capitalism.

The goal of this new type of fascism is very clear and precise: it means "total mobilization"—Ernst Jünger's term remains relevant—toward a techno-neoliberal media politics whose ferocity increases with the accelerated depletion of the planet's natural, human, and nonhuman resources. Fascism is never ambiguous, and its goals are unequivocal. The "need" for nationalist, protectionist, reactionary, and restrictive policies, for the construction of physical and discursive, mental and sensitive walls, is clarified by this goal of conducting neoliberalism to its maximum point, before "the world ends," and of making apocalypse its weapon. To do that, it needs to replace the desire for transformation with a desire for extermination: "let's end all this" as soon as possible. The State of current fascism is the State that, in its apparently anachronistic exacerbation, empties the sense of State and operationalizes the implementation of neoliberalism as the only viable politics to "save" the country from "collapse," leading the collapse toward collapse.

Under the discursive cloak of cleansing of cronyism and corrupt civil service, State policy is made to streamline as much as possible the entrepreneurship of every worker, the annulment of all labor laws, the privatization of all State-owned companies, the outsourcing of the economy, et cetera, as well as State entrepreneurship, that is, the transformation of the State into a company. This means the need to empty the sense of State through the excess of a State politics against the State.

The other need is for the State to undermine public space, for politics to undermine and empty the sense of politics, to undermine social movements and expressions of resistance, combining traditional mechanisms of torture, persecution, extermination—like in the case of Marielle Franco and many others[16]—with the promotion of the privatization and deprivation of the common space. This is done through the excess of social media, the continuous "selfization" of each individual, identified with their image for consumption, which today is not only the consumption of things but of images of things and above all of themselves. Narcissus would no longer know how to recognize himself in contemporary virtual narcissism. A verse from the chorus of Sophocles's *Antigone*, often overlooked in various analyses of this play that does not age, expresses in a concise way what

happens: "Hypsipolis, apolis" (l. 370), the excess
of polis, of politics, the emptying of the polis, of
politics. The excess of sense, the emptying of sense:
this is the rhythm of an operation of sense, which
empties sense by its exacerbation, by its hyperbole.
This is, in my view, the main driver of the new form
of fascism that afflicts and plagues us today. The
unequivocal goal of neofascism finds its method in
the ambiguation of every sense and value.

Reality today confirms that fascism lives very
well within a democratic regime, not only because
fascism is elected democratically or even because
fascism and democracy would be two sides of
the same coin, as suggested by Antonio Gramsci.
The new way of coexistence between fascism and
democracy is very clear, for example in Brazil,
partly because after decades of authoritarianism
and military dictatorship, democratic institutions
are still on the path of democratization, and partly
because in its new form, today's fascism pretends
to be more democratic than democracy.

Thus, if democracy has the representational
system as its "weak point," since many feel they
are still not represented in it, today's fascism
proclaims itself more democratic than democracy
because it exercises a power that "speaks" to each
individual "directly" via Twitter and WhatsApp, no
longer needing representatives, because democracy now wants to be the mediatic presentation of
everything that happens and not merely a representation that is never sufficiently representative.
Thus, everyone is deluded by the possibility of
direct access to inaccessible power.

Furthermore, if democracy means the power
of voting, each individual feels "empowered" by
voting continuously with their daily "likes," every
minute, for everything and everyone. More than
ever democracy shows how all political categories
are reduced to public opinion. With "likes" and
"dislikes" at every second of life, this voting serves

to continuously give the impression of a hyperactive "agency" in a democracy exercised on social media.

This equates and confuses the consumer vote with the political sense of voting, the vote as a citizen. Voting on everything all the time empties the sense of the vote when citizenship mixes with consumer activity. Citizenship is exercised as one consumes, and the right to citizenship is no longer dissociated from the right to consume. Thus, the hyperbolic vote annuls and empties the political sense of the vote. That is why today's fascism is deliriously in need of votes. Through excessive voting, the power of decision rests on the digits of the algorithmic and automatic system.

If historical fascism boasted that it achieved what no representative democracy was capable of, that is, "being" the people directly and not simply representing them, through an identification of the people with their leader or *duce*, then today social media seems to be able to finally realize this "desire," through the "direct" mediatic contact between clichés of all kinds and "each individual." Instead of the historical mobilization of the masses, "social media" attracts atomized individuals, isolated and impoverished consumers, toward connectionless connections, relationless relations, senseless senses, and valueless values.

Democracy is defined as a regime based on freedom of expression. Today's fascism wants to present itself as exercising more freedom of expression than classic liberal democracies because it has the "courage" to say what it wants in everyone's face. Rather than completely banning freedom of expression and making use of the well-known censorship mechanisms of a military dictatorship, the fascist government boasts of using the most vulgar, violent, humiliating, hateful, homophobic, racist, ordinary, and lowest words. It replaces the sense of freedom of expression with a practice of libertarianism of expression, boasting

the courage to say what the politically correct
censures within itself.

Thus, it is the politically correct that exercises
censorship, self-censorship, while fascist speech
appears as an excess of freedom of expression.
In this exacerbation of the sense of "freedom of
expression," the sense of freedom of expression is
emptied of sense. Excessive sense empties sense.
This so-called democracy that is more democratic
than democracy—new fascism—lives from the
emptying of the sense of "people" by replacing the
idea of people with their privatization and deprivation, where everything happens directly between
the environment and each individual. Today, the
people is a sample and a statistical population, the
sum of isolated atoms and atomized isolations,
brought together in networks and groups mediated
by the "virtual" and virtualized by the "medium."

For our discussion of the new form of fascism
that today surpassed the neofascism formulated
by Pasolini, it is worth noting the development of
new information technologies and the sense of
bond and connection that is operationalized in
them. Social media is the most powerful way to
achieve and establish bondless bonds, relationless
relations, and encounterless networks. It is
important to be aware that the hyperconnectivity
generated by the networks disconnects precisely
when hyperconnecting. The exacerbation of
the sense of bonds, ties, networks, connections—"links," "networks"—empties, by excess,
the sense of relation. It is the hyperbole of the
sense of relation that empties the sense of relation
and the relation of senses.

With this, the *in-between*-us—the open space
of the common, more decisive for a living and
free politics than any demarcation of a common
space—is seen to be privatized and private,
because the opposite of in-between is not together
but hyperpolarization. Also, the space of solitude

of each one, the space of creation, is privatized
and private because it is confused with the
isolation that includes or excludes each one from
the market and its images. With the pandemic,
these and many other issues discussed here have
become more acute.

The new fascism continues to exercise the
age-old boundaries of every totalitarianism: *divide
et impera*, divide and conquer, and also *panem
et circenses*, bread and circuses. The difference
is that it intensifies them by making them
ambiguous, because today fascism unites in order
to divide and thus stimulate even more evidently
so that each citizen should voluntarily serve the
tyrant—the neoliberalization of all systems—and
that every bread becomes a circus, that is, every
reality, especially that of the breadwinner,
becomes a spectacle.

Thus, democracy is dissolving as if "naturally"
(which today means the same as "artificially") not
by decree or institutional act (although several acts
and decrees are also being voted in parliaments
while media scandals occupy the front pages)
but while being preserved as an empty form by
the growing disarticulation and the continuous
dissolution of the common and of the practices of
inclusion. The viralization that disseminates and
thus exacerbates senses not only empties them
but also operationalizes the naturalization of all
types of discourse, especially hate and exclusion
discourses within this senseless hollow.

The linguistic mechanisms for naturalizing
racism and exclusive segregation studied so carefully by Victor Klemperer in his important work
*The Language of the Third Reich: LTI—Lingua Tertii
Imperii*[17] find today in social media and in the
robotic algorithm of messages a means of uncon-
trollable naturalization. Through "humor" and viral
"jokes" in memes and messages, hatred starts to
become as natural as the artifices of its production.

The "loss of linguistic ability" observed by Pasolini as a sign of televisual neofascism is now going viral and becoming naturalized by the continuous production of new words and expressions through which the unacceptable becomes the most natural.

What Pasolini had seen as the event of "something" happening and what he witnessed with the disappearance of fireflies from the Italian landscape becomes more and more explicit as the universal event of *every* thing, sense, and value transforming into *any* thing, into *any* sense and *any* value, emptying both the senses and values of things as well as the sense and value of sense and value. This is what we may call the "anyzation" of each thing.[18] With that, the sense of each and every one, the sense of the singular, dissipates, since *each one* is now confused with *anybody*.

This is what the advancement of information technologies, the development of artificial intelligence, of the numerical society manages to naturalize and thus universalize and totalize. The thesis I would like to outline is that the "unpredictably new" form of fascism we are witnessing today is the form of the ambiguity of all forms. It is a fascism that is articulated in the ambiguity and oscillation of all sense and value in such a way that in this oscillating ambiguity, sense and value lose value and sense. Ambiguity here means emptying, by making every sense equivalent to any sense. It is because of this ambiguous oscillation and oscillating ambiguity where all formulas and expressions can be inverted and perverted, where every sense and value can be turned against itself and against any other, that not only the "voluntary servitude" of everyone to the tyranny of a unity that annihilates all living unity—evoking the classic concept and discussions of Étienne de La Boétie published clandestinely in 1577[19]—but also the new mechanisms of power, control, and censorship become possible.

It is this dynamic of sense that I am calling here
the fascism of ambiguity.

The fascism of the ambiguity of every sense
and value is found everywhere today. At any
moment and in any situation, we see senses oscillating between right and wrong, true and false in
a growing ambiguity that, in an astonishing way,
shows how even the polarization of senses, values,
and positions triggers the ambiguity of senses
more than their distinction and demarcation. The
very oscillation of the sense of "fascism" testifies
to the continuous ambiguation of senses: How to
speak of fascism if today's *duci* are nothing but
caricatures of past fascists, parodies of dictators?
A terrifying example is the case of Russia's
fascism, where the very use of the word becomes
a powerful weapon for reanimating the phantoms
of the past. By using the term "fascism" to build
hate speech to justify, legitimate, and enable
murder, the regime turns "anti-fascism" into a
new form of fascist discourse and practice.

Everywhere there are caricatures of caricatures, idolatries of idolatries, masks of masks,
parodies of parodies, all intentionally staged in
autopilot mode, which allows us to say that they
are both caricatures and noncaricatures, both
masks and nonmasks, fascism, anti-fascism,
and democracy. After all, in the world of images,
where everything is what it is not and what
is not is what is, nonbeing presents itself as
nonbeing and not as what is hidden behind being;
everything is by definition ambiguous, one of the
faces of Janus, the two-faced face. In the world of
ambiguous oscillation and the oscillating ambiguity of senses, which is the world of the image of
the image, nothing is hidden; everything is shown
and shown in everyone's face, including the hiding
of senses and intentions. What seems particularly
terrifying is that the fascism of ambiguity aims to
erase the very need for a practice of senses when

the very sense of searching for meaning becomes
meaningless and truth is not merely covered and
disguised but loses its own veracity.

Translated from the Portuguese by Rodrigo Maltez Novaes

1   Timothy Snyder, "We Should Say It: Russia Is Fascist," *The New York Times*, May 19, 2022, https://www.nytimes.com/2022/05/19/opinion/russia-fascism-ukraine-putin.html, accessed November 22, 2022.

2   Marcia Sá Cavalcante Schuback, *The Fascism of Ambiguity: A Conceptual Essay*, trans. Rodrigo Maltez Novaes (New York: Bloomsbury, 2022).

3   Benito Mussolini, *Fascism: Doctrine and Institutions* (New York: Howard Fertig, 1968), p. 15.

4   Ernst Jünger, "Total Mobilization," trans. Joel Golb and Richard Wolin, in *The Heidegger Controversy*, ed. Richard Wolin (Cambridge, MA: MIT Press, 1993), pp. 119–39.

5   Karl Marx and Friedrich Engels, *The German Ideology: Including Theses on Feuerbach and Introduction to the Critique of Political Economy* (Amherst, NY: Prometheus Books, 1998).

6   Mussolini, *Fascism* (see note 3), p. 19.

7   Ibid.

8   Ibid., pp. 19–20.

9   Ibid., p. 23.

10 Pier Paolo Pasolini, *Saggi sulla politica e sulla società* (Milan: Mondadori, 1999), p. 407. Unless otherwise noted, all translations are by Rodrigo Maltez Novaes.

11 Ibid., p. 1530.

12 Ibid., pp. 336–43.

13 Ibid., p. 1457.

14 Ibid., pp. 358, 1269.

15 Georges Didi-Huberman, *Survival of the Fireflies*, trans. Lia Swope Mitchell (Minneapolis: University of Minnesota Press, 2018). Even before Didi-Huberman, Nancy Mangabeira Unger, without even knowing Pasolini's texts, had already discussed the "perplexity of fireflies" in *O encantamento do humano: Ecologia e espiritualidade* (São Paulo: Edições Loyola, 1991).

16 Marielle Franco, born 1979, was a Black Brazilian politician, sociologist, feminist, and human rights activist murdered through several gun shots on March 14, 2018 in Rio de Janeiro.

17 Victor Klemperer, *The Language of the Third Reich: LTI—Lingua Tertii Imperii; A Philologist's Notebook*, trans. Martin Brady (New York: Continuum, 2006).

18 In some previous texts, I suggested the verb "to whatsoever," "whatsoevering." But maybe "anyzation" can render my point more clearly here. See "The Lacuna of Hermeneutics," *Research in Phenomenology* 51 (2021): pp. 165–77.

19 Étienne de La Boétie, *The Politics of Obedience: The Discourse of Voluntary Servitude*, trans. Harry Kurz (New York: Free Life Editions, 1975).

Fascism as the Death Drive of Empire

Oxana Timofeeva

115

On April 1, 2022, horrifying photos from the city of Bucha in the Kyiv region of Ukraine permeated the international media. The photos were made after a one-month occupation by the Russian military and bore abundant testimony to the terrible massacres its soldiers committed during this time. Many bodies of civilians, including those of women and children, were found dead, mutilated, and burnt, with bound hands, with traces of torture and rape. There were corpses everywhere on the streets, in the basements, but also in mass graves hastily dug by the soldiers to hide the evidence of their atrocities.

How did the Russian official media react to these images? They called them a provocation and claimed that Ukrainians had simply staged the killings and faked footage in order to discredit the Russian armed forces. In addition, on April 18, the 64th Separate Guards Motor Rifle Brigade, which had operated in Bucha, was decorated with the honor guard status by President Vladimir Putin. This case showed that genocide, torture, and mass murder are still possible in the 21st century on the European continent. Moreover, those committing such crimes can be celebrated as national heroes.

From the geopolitical perspective, shared by many right-wingers, war is war, and everything can happen there. The state of exception normalizes violence as the means justified by certain ends, such as interests of sovereign states and alliances. From the moral point of view, prevalent in liberal media, what happened in Bucha is pure evil and thus defies rational explanation. The general problem with evil, however, is that, in the eyes of the one who judges, it always comes from the Other, in whose face they would never recognize their own. The syllogism of moral consciousness—"I could never do that; others are people like me; therefore, Bucha is not possible"—breaks down due to the fact that it is not only possible but actual and real. If Russian military personnel are people like me, how could they torture noncombatants, kill children, or rape women and then burn them? The easiest solution would be to dehumanize the criminals and search for the roots of their pathological obsession with cruelty in the national character or the Russian culture, notorious for its tendencies to celebrate violence. Then comes the next syllogism: "Others are human beings like me; Russian soldiers are not like me; therefore, they are not human beings."

Leaving behind both of these popular perspectives—geopolitical cynicism, which justifies war crimes, on the one hand, and liberal moral consciousness, which dehumanizes their perpetrators, on the other—I suggest taking a different approach. To comprehend Bucha as reality, together with the conditions of its possibility, we have to look beyond good and evil, into the depths of what the ancients used to call the human soul, or what psychoanalysis calls the unconscious. From that perspective, Bucha is not an exception or a scandal in itself. It is rather but one of the names for something that constantly repeats itself in the history of humanity, regardless of the level of progress in this or that particular geographical area. This outcome is always one of the possible developments of war, after the tragedies of the 20th century, and it can thus be associated with fascist aggression but not necessarily reduced to it. It is this phenomenon that provides the theater of war with its most terrifying scenes.

The theater of war (*Kriegstheater, theatrum belli*) is a term popularized by Carl von Clausewitz, and it is very precise: reality itself is a theater, where actions develop according to a certain scenario written by no one, with scenes of violence and death rehearsed and repeated beyond our volition.

118

If war is theater, Bucha is a scene—not in the sense implied by the Russian propaganda machine, but in a much more radical sense: what happens when we look at the images of tortured and murdered people is a phantasmatic encounter between the one who looks and what is looked at. There are scenes that provoke horror or repulsion, scenes that we would like to unsee, that we immediately tend to replace with something more acceptable.

The psychological mechanism of negation works to repress the contents of such unbearable scenes. From a psychoanalytical perspective, these contents are extremely important for understanding a subject's inner truth, their unconscious desires and drives. Bucha can be regarded as a distorted mirror in which today's humanity cannot recognize itself, looking at its own frightening projection of the inhuman Other as a source of evil. The scene of Bucha displays—to borrow Slavoj Žižek's words—"the cause of the terror constitutive of our being-human, the inhuman core of being-human, the dimension of what the German Idealists called negativity and Freud called the death drive."[1]

The death drive (*Todestrieb*) is a controversial concept first introduced by Sabina Spielrein, a Russian physician and psychoanalyst later killed by the Nazis in Rostov-on-Don in 1942. In her essay "Destruction as the Cause of Coming into Being" (1912), she claims that human sexuality has two components, reproductive and destructive, and suggests the idea of the death drive as subordinate to the reproductive drive.[2] Sigmund Freud elaborates on this concept in *Beyond the Pleasure Principle* (1920) but turns it upside down. According to Freud, Thanatos is not only a drive in its own right but actually dominates Eros.

Freud points out that patients returning from World War I with traumatic neuroses, today called "post-traumatic stress disorder" (PTSD), often have recurring dreams whose content refers to their real negative experiences "bringing the patient back into the situation of his accident, a situation from which he wakes up in another fright." Note that Freud believed in "the wish-fulfilling tenor of dreams."[3] What kind of wish can be fulfilled in such a roundabout way? Apparently, the disposition of desire that is at stake here differs from mere searching for pleasures. After exploring some possible positivist explanations of the compulsion to repeat, Freud makes a speculative suggestion that there must be "something that seems more primitive, more elementary, more instinctual than the pleasure principle which it overrides." This primitive instinct is conservative and points to "an urge inherent in organic life to restore an earlier state of things," that is, to return to the state of an inorganic nature.[4] Rarely does the death drive reach consciousness, but rather it comes in disguise, camouflaged in all sorts of desires. However, in some cases, it crops up. War is such a case.

In Freud's letter to Albert Einstein titled "Why War?" (1933), another aspect of the death drive comes to the fore: that of aggression. There are two kinds of instincts, he writes: "those which seek to preserve and unite—which we call 'erotic,' exactly in the sense in which Plato uses the word 'Eros' in his *Symposium*, or 'sexual,' with a deliberate extension of the popular conception of 'sexuality'—and those which seek to destroy and kill and which we group together as the aggressive or destructive instinct."[5] Freud is referring to such well-known opposites as love and hate, or attraction and repulsion, and he emphasizes that these two drives are alloyed and interdependent. In fact, we cannot really isolate one from the other. This is why war always has its followers: the road to hell is paved with good intentions; the passion for destruction operates under the guise of state patriotism, religion, or other positive values. As Freud writes,

when human beings are incited to war they
may have a whole number of motives for
assenting—some noble and some base, some
which are openly declared and others which
are never mentioned. . . . A lust for aggression
and destruction is certainly among them: the
countless cruelties in history and in everyday
lives vouch for its existence and its strength.
The satisfaction of these destructive impulses
is of course facilitated by their admixture with
others of an erotic and idealistic kind. When
we read of the atrocities of the past, it sometimes seems as though the idealistic motives
served only as an excuse for the destructive
appetites; and sometimes—in the case, for
instance, of the cruelties of the Inquisition—it
seems as though the idealistic motives had
pushed themselves forward in consciousness,
while the destructive ones lent them an unconscious reinforcement.[6]

The destructive impulse, which finds its release
at war, is not the death drive itself, but rather a
result of a complex process of its inversion: "The
death instinct turns into the destructive instinct
when, with the help of special organs, it is directed
outwards, on to objects. The organism preserves
its own life, so to say, by destroying an extraneous
one."[7] In this perspective, war can be understood
as a collective Thanatos redirected toward another
people. Conscious motives are just a surface
element of a complex apparatus fueled by the
unconscious death drive of an aggressor.

While the concept of the death drive is
contested as too speculative and counterintuitive,
the hard data of ongoing atrocities proves Freud
right. However, to understand the scene of Bucha
in its singularity, a simple gesture of applying
psychoanalytic theory to the empirical data would
not be sufficient. It only gives us a general sense of

why this scene causes us such horror and rejection. Yes, it is a mirror, but a mirror of what? In other words, who or what is the subject of the death drive appearing onstage in Bucha?

Emp i re

On April 19 (that is, shortly after Bucha), Russian writer Aleksandr Nikonov received a phone call from the actor Ivan Okhlobystin, known for his ultraconservative and pro-Putin views. The actor was drunk. Apparently, he was ringing all of his friends for a farewell of sorts, reporting his willingness to go to Ukraine to fight for Putin (he never went there in the end). Nikonov recorded the conversation and shared it online as truly representative of the current state of mind of all Russian "patriots." Here are some excerpts from Okhlobystin's speech:

> Russia will always win. We will win! . . . Even if the impossible happens and we lose, it means that the whole world will lose with us. Nothing will happen! There will be a great Zero. And we are all ready for this Apocalypse! All people agree. And you have no idea to what extent! In unison! . . . We will kill everyone! We do not need a world in which there is no our victory [sic], Putin did not say this in vain. . . .[8]

In this excitement in the face of death, the death drive manifests itself in its pure form. One can indeed qualify it as a case of psychosis, as much individual as collective: apocalyptic dreams of the pro-government intelligentsia are performed by the militaries as real actors of the theater of war in their *passage à l'acte* in the bloody scene of Bucha. My intention is not, however, to diagnose other people, be they famous actors or no-name soldiers. It is easy to offer treatments to others from the position of moral superiority but much harder to muster the courage to look into the mirror, to register oneself with regards to the reality of Bucha, which is reflected in the eyes of human beings, including the "good" and the "normal" ones.

My focus is on the death drive operating not in any war whatsoever, but in a specific historical situation of an imperialism now collapsing into fascism. This is the case of my country, and my people. It is not particularly new. Something similar happened in other countries before and will most probably happen again elsewhere. Like a traumatic neurotic's dream, Bucha is a recurring scene. We can try to forget it, to forbid it, but it returns under different names breaking through the invocation "never again," because it is not an isolated phenomenon but a phantasmatic exercise of a certain psychosocial composition whose invariance must be analyzed and called into question if we really want to not only get rid of a symptom (bad dreams) but liberate ourselves from their causes.

Although many people today object to comparisons between Vladimir Putin's Russia, Adolf Hitler's Germany, or Benito Mussolini's Italy, I insist on a certain structural homology between these regimes, for which fascism can work as a generic term. Thus, among the basic elements they share, one is crucial to my further argument: a nostalgia for some great empire of the past. This nostalgia cultivates the feeling of a nation's ethnic, religious, cultural, or other superiority. Meanwhile, its political ethos is reduced to imagining wars of conquest, restoring the glory of the old days, and dominating over other groups and territories. So, there is a connection between imperialism and fascism, but it is not direct: not every claim toward the restoration of an old empire is necessarily pregnant with fascist or protofascist ideology. I will try to grasp this indirect connection in philosophical terms by referring to Georg Wilhelm Friedrich Hegel's dialectics, wherein empire is presented not so much as a political unit but as a state of mind.

In chapter 6 of his *Phenomenology of Spirit*, Hegel introduces the history of Western civilization in three consecutive stages: A. True Spirit, Ethical Life; B. Spirit Alienated from Itself; C. Spirit Certain of Itself: Morality.[9] Ethics here is inseparable from politics. For Hegel, the question of ethics is not one of the abstract good and evil, but of concrete practices. These are the only ways for what he calls "spirit" to realize itself in the world. According to Jean Hyppolite's commentary, this chapter examines "particular spirits," that is, historical-political formations: "that of the Greek city, that of the Roman Empire and Roman law, that of Western culture, that of the French Revolution, and that of the Germanic world."[10]

The true spirit of the *Phenomenology*'s section A corresponds to the Greek city (polis), which is not yet a state but a municipal community. A happy people live there in a harmonic balance of two competing laws: the human law (male, rational, social) and the divine one (female, unconscious, familial). The ethical life of the city, however, is limited by other cities that live according to other laws, and this is how it comes to an end: engaging in wars, people reassemble in a state of legality, which corresponds to the Roman Empire and Roman law. Section B—Spirit, Alienated from Itself—presents the so-called cultural formation as the dialectics of noble and base consciousness, where the feudal nobility cannot really find its place between state power and wealth. In the mode of Enlightenment, a reluctant educated class drifts toward revolution, that is, the overthrow of absolutism. Revolution is thought as an ultimate negativity, but at the same time as a necessary step to freedom. It first emerges as a purely negative force—terror, guillotine, and

the triumph of death—but then develops into a
moral universe of true equality. Only after the revolution, according to Hegel's *Phenomenology*, does
the true state emerge—not as a city in the Greek
sense, not as an empire, which tends to despotism,
and not as a monarchy, where the sovereignty is
supported by the language of flattery, but as a state
of mutual recognition, a moral universe of forgive-
ness and reconciliation.

The problem with this conception is
that it presents one particular narrative as a
universal history, which, indeed, now qualifies
as a Eurocentric approach. We should note,
however, that in the respective chapters of the
Phenomenology, Hegel does not really mention
the Roman Empire, the French Revolution, and
so on. All these names and indications come from
authoritative commentaries. One of the most
famous of them belongs to Alexandre Kojève, who
claims that after the French Revolution, world
history ends with the establishment of the homo-
geneous state of mutual recognition and absolute
knowing. Although he suggested several versions
of the actual location of the end of the world—the
US, Russia, Europe, Japan—Kojève believed that
this state is already achieved, and even if it is now
still geographically limited, it will gradually spread
through the world and less progressive countries
will develop in accordance with the general model
(such as today's EU).[11]

Today, the empirical data seems to refute
Kojève's interpretation: neither the American way
of life nor European liberal democracy, neither
capitalist globalization nor anything else has
proved potent enough to homogenize the world
and bring it to the point of mutual recognition,
which, first and foremost, would mean true
equality (and not just a formal one). Nevertheless,
the same empirical data does not refute Hegel's
theory itself, insofar as his dialectics proves to be

applicable to various historical phenomena and is not necessarily reduced to the Roman Empire, the French Revolution, or Europe in general. Without naming particular "spirits," Hegel allows us to read "Roman Empire" or "French Revolution" as concrete historical examples of a certain repeatable logic, a scenario that can be performed on different stages, played by different actors—where each variation will be different. What Hegel writes is not really history but phenomenology, and the sixth chapter can be summarized as a dialectics of the city, the empire, and the state, which are unraveled as consecutive forms of consciousness.

I will focus on one of these episodes, a fragment on the empire, which, in my perspective, is crucial for understanding the trouble we are in, although it is very short, just a few pages, in contrast to the long preceding section on the Greek polis. Hegel's reader can feel how all of his sympathies are on the side of the ethical life of the polis. This is the world of the characters of Greek tragedies. Each one is an individual who acts according to human (written) or divine (unwritten) law. Individuality is concrete insofar as it is performed in the name of something substantial, for instance, family, religion, community, or tradition: every character has such a background that pervades them. It is called pathos. Thus, Antigone consciously transgresses human law for the sake of divine law and takes the blame upon herself for illicitly burying her brother Polynices. Her pathos is sisterhood, pure feminine love, both unconscious and divine.

The passage between the polis and the empire is designated by war. The warrior, the young man, leaves his Penates, his family, and, more generally, breaks his immanent connection to the world of the feminine for the sake of the external polity. Thus, he becomes ethically independent "from all existence," that is, from his background, from any positive content, which is replaced by negative freedom:

> War is the spirit and the form in which the essential moment of ethical substance, the absolute *freedom* of ethically *independent beings* from all existence, is present in its actuality and in having proved itself. While, on the one hand, war makes the single *systems* of property and personal self-sufficiency as well as singular *personality* itself feel the force of the negative, in war this negative essence otherwise brings itself to the forefront as what sustains the whole.[12]

Something very important is lost in this rise of the masculine culture of warfare, whence imperialism grows out of. In the section "The State of Legality," Hegel describes this loss as the vanishing of the spirit that, in ethical life, comprised the concrete unity of individuality with its substance, such as family ties or native land. As the cities cannot really hold together, the empire finally subordinates their multiplicity to the abstract unity of the juridical law. Unlike the human and divine laws of the Greek city, this law is universally applicable and imposes a formal equality. Its subjects are not characters with their pathos but persons in the legal sense, detached from any substantial positivity: "The universal is splintered into the atoms of absolutely multiple individuals; this spirit, having died, is an *equality* in which *all* count for as much as *each* and where each and all count as *persons*."[13]

A person of the Roman law appears as self-sufficient, but sooner or later every reader of Hegel learns that nothing in the world is self-sufficient, and all exists insofar as it is involved in processes of interaction. Personhood in a formal sense reduces individuals to the state of legality. It is an

127

abstract and empty "one," "a contingent existence, an essenceless movement and doing that never reaches any kind of stable existence." The only stable existence to which it can relate is property. As an abstract person, I am nobody, but there are things that are mine. This would be fine, but as what I am, I cannot really identify with what I have: "The actual content, or the *determinateness* of something's being mine—whether it be an external possession or else that of either inner richness or a poverty of both spirit and character—is not contained in this empty form and does not concern it."[14] I can try to reach a certain stability surrounding myself with more and more things, but I myself will remain no-thing, nothing substantial.

This section presents a deep and at the same time very concise analysis of a mechanism that underlies the entire social structure of capitalist modernity. Indeed, private property existed before, but, in Hegel's perspective, what makes it truly constitutive is Roman law, before which everybody is formally equal but absolutely precarious. You are (not) what you own: this could be the formula of alienation, which gives rise to the donut hole of modern subjectivity. In the following paragraphs (480–81), Hegel presents his insights into mass psychology and introduces a very interesting new figure, closely related to the abstract person: the lord of the world. This figure is a collective projection. It emerges when "the absolute *plurality* of atoms of personality is … equally collected into a *single* and equally spiritless point alien to them." The lord of the world is not a "higher type of spirit."[15] He is a person, too, but an absolute one, in the sense that he embodies and at the same time confronts all other persons as their alienated content and essence.

As noted by Hyppolite: "The period between the reign of Augustus and that of Alexander Severus (250 A.D.) is considered to be the great era of legal science. But it is also the period of the most ruthless domination, a period in the course of which all the ancient civic and religious institutions died out as despotism grew."[16] What Hegel shows here is how atomized people create the phantasmatic figure of a despot out of their own emptiness, determined by ownership. In turn, this aggregative figure itself is empty, as it is assembled from multiple empty ones. The people think that the despot is an authority external to them and do not realize their deep affinity to him. Meanwhile, it is exclusively upon their worship and fear that his power actually rests: "This lord of the world, cognizant of himself as the epitome of all actual powers, is a monstrous self-consciousness who knows himself as an actual god. However, since he is only the formal self who is unable to bring those powers under control, his emotional life and his self-indulgence are equally monstrous excesses."[17]

As the lord of the world is a gigantic empty self that does not have any positive content, he can only manifest himself as "destructive violence, which he exercises upon the selves of his subjects as they confront him." He is a negative embodiment of the social alienation itself:

> Those persons are thus in an only negative relationship to each other in the same way that they are in a negative relationship to the lord of the world, who is himself their relation to each other, or their continuity with each other. As this continuity, he is the essence and content of their formalism, but he is a content alien to them, a hostile essence who sublates what counts for them as their essence, namely, their contentless being-for-itself—and as the continuity of their personality, he destroys that very personality itself.[18]

We, as persons, might fear the despot or oppose ourselves to him, and conceive him as an external force which we cannot control, but what we forget is that in this fabric of social estrangement we create him out of our own spiritless existence fully subordinated to the relations of property. Despotism is the obscene flip side of the abstract individualism of the state of empire and—to return to my initial point—its death drive, personalized in the figure of the lord of the world.

In the next section, "B. Spirit Alienated from Itself," Hegel describes how empire degrades into feudal monarchy, where aristocracy feeds the vanity of the sovereign, but the growth of the education level and the spread of Enlightenment ideas make it clear that the king is naked. Revolution destroys imperial power and absolutism and gives rise to a new form of consciousness, the moral one, which corresponds to the state of the real (and not only formal) equality among people, who find their spirit and substance in their new consciously and freely created community. In *The Phenomenology of Spirit*, history ends here, and it looks like a happy end. Further, alternative developments are not taken into account, prompting commentators such as Alexandre Kojève with his strong Eurocentric vision of the one and only version of world history to present this point as the ultimate accomplishment of Hegel's spirit.

Fascism

In a more conventional reading, the Greek polis, the Roman Empire, the French Revolution, or the German state are rather conceptual models, and similar stories could be repeated elsewhere. In this regard, I agree with Hyppolite's claim that the description of the state of legality and the lord of the world "has a historical reference (it corresponds to the moment of the Roman Empire), but

it also has a more general bearing."[19] It is not only
the story of the Roman Empire but, in a sense, our
own story too. Thus, we have never been Romans,
but Russia has its own imperial legacy, of which
one element recently emerged as if out of the blue:
the figure of the despot who thinks of himself
as the lord of the world, and who exercises his
own contentless empty self in purely destructive
actions. Back in 2020, when, after being in power
for twenty years, Putin changed the Russian consti-
tution to get a life-long presidency, I was thinking
that, as long as his autocratic governance tended
to degrade into a kind of neofeudal monarchy, the
new revolution in Russia was just a matter of time.
However, I did not consider another possibility for
this regime to save itself: instead of a revolution,
we got war. Moreover, what seemed to be a typical
manifestation of autocratic governance among
many others rapidly took a fascist turn.

"Behind every fascism there is a failed revolution": this famous sentence is often attributed
to Walter Benjamin, although it is not a direct
quote but rather an interpretation of some of his
fragments. Thus, in "The Work of Art in the Age
of Mechanical Reproduction," Benjamin states:
"Fascism attempts to organize the newly prole-
tarianized masses without affecting the property
structure which the masses strive to eliminate."[20]
In the same vein, in "The Psychological Structure
of Fascism," Georges Bataille characterizes
fascism as "an imperative response to the growing
threat of a working class movement."[21] Both
authors claim that fascism emerges as a means
to neutralize the growing social antagonism by
creating a national unity of the oppressors and the
oppressed around one strong leader. It recanalizes
the energy of revolution into military aggression
toward an external enemy.

Basically, we can say that fascism functions
in accordance with the mechanism that Freud

revealed as the death drive at the origins of war: instead of letting itself be demolished by the storm of revolution, a given form of power and property relations calling itself a nation tries to preserve itself and find another object for its (self-)destructive impulses. The great empire of the past, which a national leader calls to restore, corresponds to "an earlier state of things" to which the death drive urges us to return to—a chthonic deity of Mother Earth as both a uterus and a grave where one would finally rest in peace. Okhlobystin's exclamation that "We do not need a world in which there is no our victory" is nothing but a record of this agony of empire that desperately struggles with its own desire to die in the flames of revolution. Hegel writes on the necessity of revolution, but—unlike Karl Marx—he does not discuss the idea of changing property relations. However, his own analysis suggests that these relations create an existential condition for the dialectics of abstract personhood and the lord of the world, which make revolutions fail and renders imperialist politics so sustainable. After a series of revolutions, we are still not living in the universal state of mutual recognition but in imperialist states controlled by men of property, where the excess of despotism is always a possibility and a lord of the world can always become a *Führer*.

According to Bataille, fascism is the ultimate concentration of royal or imperial authority in the unity of religion and army. Therefore, the analysis of the mechanisms of sovereign power must constitute "the foundation of any coherent description of fascism." The figure of the sovereign, which Bataille defines as "the imperative form of heterogeneous existence," is an element of a complex sociopsychological structure. Heterogeneous here means that the sovereign is not really a part of the society, which tends toward heterogeneity, mainly represented by the class of owners—the bourgeoisie. He is an extraordinary figure, outside, above, but also in the center of this structure. On the periphery, there are heterogeneous elements too. However, this is another heterogeneity, not of the sovereign, but of the lowest classes and social outcasts. This other heterogeneity is a pole of fluctuations and unrest that threatens the regular bourgeois order of the homogenous part of the society. Fascism begins from the process of mobilization, when the imperative figure becomes the central point of affective attraction aimed at neutralizing dangerous movements from the periphery by pushing them toward homogeneity: "In fundamental opposition to socialism, fascism is characterized by the uniting of classes."[22]

Two aspects are crucial for the structure of fascism: the religious and the military. By religious aspect Bataille means the social function of the sacred, which is based on the constant movement of differentiation between two poles: on the one hand, there are the highest values, the sacralized purity, and the glory of power, and on the other, the ignoble, dirty, accursed elements. The specificity of fascism consists in this possibility of mobilizing this negative part of the sacred world, embodied by the heterogeneous part of society: "Fascism's close ties with the impoverished classes profoundly distinguish this formation from classical royal society, which is characterized by a more or less decisive loss of contact with the lower classes." In fact, in fascism, this most dangerous and precarious peripheral part becomes the main support of the imperative authority, insofar as it becomes mobilized and forms the body of the army: the soldiers "belong as a rule to a vile segment of the population."[23]

Let me give you an example of the Russian army. In peacetime, there are generally two types of soldiers: conscript and contract soldiers. Only contract soldiers (including those working for private armies) can engage in real fighting, also called "special military operations." A great number of contract soldiers come from the poorest regions and families—these are people who would consider killing or being killed for a decent salary as an option for survival. Conscripts do regular military service and cannot legally be ordered to fight. However, they can be forced to sign a contract. In Russia, young boys from rich and middle-class families, whose parents have enough money to pay corrupt army functionaries, usually have legal excuses to avoid conscription. Therefore, most conscripts also come from depressed social backgrounds. In wartime, with the announcement of mobilization, everyone can become a soldier (with a few exceptions). But, again, the social stratification is preserved: first, people from peripheral regions once colonized by the Russian Empire—such as Buryatia, Yakutia, Tuva, Chuvashia, Kalmykia, Dagestan, and others—are thrown into the furnace of war, whereas privileged men from the central areas escape mobilization. This fits into Bataille's scheme, which explains the miracle of fascism quite well: the more dispossessed the masses are, the more they support the state apparatuses.

While the state of legality described by Hegel is based on the dialectics of the lord of the world and an abstract person, that is, anybody taken as nobody, the fascist state of illegality, into which imperial power collapses when it tries to preserve itself, develops in between the two poles of chief and soldier. On the one hand, the army is associated with the nobility and glory of the sovereign authority, on the other, with bloodshed, carnage, and death. These opposites are united by the mechanisms of their identification and attraction:

The affective character of this unification is manifest in the form of the soldier's attachment to the head of the army: it implies that each soldier equates the latter's glory with his own. This process is the intermediary through which disgusting slaughter is radically transformed into its opposite, glory, namely into a pure and intense attraction. The glory of the chief essentially constitutes a sort of affective pole opposed to the nature of the soldiers.[24]

This offers us insight into the sense of Bucha: the more elevated the figure of the chief, the more ignoble is the slaughter providing the affective charge of the sacrality of his status. The chief and his soldiers create a dynamic unity, which, as Hegel would say, manifests itself as monstrosity and destructive violence.

Bataille's deeper philosophical explanation of this mechanism is in fact very similar to Hegel's analysis of how the lord of the world destroys the personality of the abstract person:

> Human beings incorporated into the army are but negated elements, negated with a kind of rage (a sadism), manifest in the tone of each command, negated by the parade, by the uniform, and by the geometric regularity of cadenced movements. The chief, insofar as he is imperative, is the incarnation of this violent negation. His intimate nature, the nature of his glory, is constituted by an imperative act that annuls the wretched populace (which constitutes the army) as such.[25]

The Limits of Growth

In January 2022, I was walking the streets of St. Petersburg and observing numerous new residential districts under construction. Looking at these multistory estates rapidly replacing the old low-rise housing, I was trying to imagine how many families were to settle in these human anthills. The city is congested, the world is overpeopled, I thought. Our species is drastically expanding.

Populations, communities, organisms, economies, or any other system can experience growth. All these kinds of growth are organized according to the same logic. As Bataille argued in his remarkable book *The Accursed Share*, the growth of an individual or a system results from it receiving an excessive amount of energy. The first-ever original source of energy is the sun, which dispenses light and warmth and thus provides for all life on Earth. Plants consume solar energy and do nothing but grow and reproduce. Reproduction in this sense is just the next level of growth. A plant vegetates and, when it is big enough, blossoms and produces offspring. First comes a tree, then a forest. An animal consumes plants or other animals that consume plants, grows bigger in size, and when it reaches sexual maturation, finds a partner and procreates: "In a sense, reproduction signifies a passage from individual growth to that of a group."[26]

There are, however, limits to growth. Another individual or a group can be the limit to my growth, but the only real limit, according to Bataille, is the terrestrial sphere, or biosphere, that is, the space available for life. Therefore, there is a rotation on Earth: an individual or population eventually vanishes to give room to newcomers. Death is nature's means to restore the balance, to put an end to the process of the growth of the living: "If one considers life as a whole, there is not really growth but a maintenance of volume in general."[27]

Moreover, on the planetary level destruction prevails over production. Any possible growth can be understood as a compensation for the general processes of destruction that living individuals do not control. Such is the opposition, introduced by Bataille, between general and restricted economies: restricted, or human, economy is aimed at growth, accumulation, and production, whereas the general, or planetary, economy demands nonproductive expenditures. In this sense, death, like sexual reproduction, is an exuberance of organic nature that canalizes its excessive energies into luxurious destruction: "The luxury of death is regarded by us in the same way as that of sexuality, first as a negation of ourselves, then—in a sudden reversal—as the profound truth of that movement of which life is the manifestation."[28]

This is Bataille's own version of the death drive, where death and sexuality belong to the same element. Its driving force is not a libidinal energy in the Freudian sense but an excessive planetary or, ultimately, solar energy. Roughly speaking, behind every erotic impulse of living individuals that try to grow and reproduce, there is a Thanatos of luxurious destruction that connects them to the level of the universe. Bataille summarizes his argument in the following way: "If the system can no longer grow, or if the excess cannot be completely absorbed in its growth, it must necessarily be lost without profit; it must be spent, willingly or not, gloriously or catastrophically."[29]

Hence his reply to the same question, which Freud discussed with Einstein in 1932: "Why War?" According to Bataille, modern war in general is a catastrophic consequence of ignoring the necessity of nonproductive expenditure. The growth of human restrictive economies, and in particular capitalist economy, results in an accumulation of excessive wealth. To spend it gloriously and willingly would mean to share, to give without reciprocation. This would imply redistribution of wealth toward more equality and establishing an economy of gifts, incommensurate with capitalist greed. Instead, capitalist humanity spends its excessive wealth catastrophically. War comes as

an unconscious fulfillment of the planetary death
drive. In an instant, an army can ruin a city or
an entire country, built for years or centuries,
ruin thousands or even millions of lives. One can
rationalize or justify war by referring to geopolitical
interests of certain states, groups, and coalitions,
but these rationalizations will always remain all-too-
human. On the planetary level, war is a pure waste.

In this maximally distant perspective, my idea
of fascism as the death drive of the empire can be
formulated in yet another way. According to Freud,
might suggests that a nation tries to preserve itself
by transforming its death drive into military aggression, but according to Bataille, on a bigger planetary
level the state of empire simply meets the limits of
growth and, pretending that it wants to preserve
itself and destroy the other, unconsciously tries to
waste itself. In other words, what presents itself as
an attempt to restore the Russian Empire is in fact
the reality of its collapse. Insofar as our own phantasmatic, monstrous projection, acting as a supreme
authority, destroys us under the pretext of destroying our neighbors, there is nothing to preserve here,
but also nothing to lose as we are negated—first as
abstract individuals in an empire or quasi-empire,
then as soldiers in a fascist army—by the one who
thinks of himself as lord of the world.

1 Slavoj Žižek, *Less than Nothing: Hegel and the Shadow of Dialectical Materialism* (London: Verso, 2012), p. 830.

2 Sabina Spielrein, "Destruction as the Cause of Coming into Being," *Journal of Analytic Psychology* 39 (1994): pp. 155–86.

3 *The Standard Edition of the Complete Psychological Works of Sigmund Freud*, trans. and ed. James Strachey, vol. 18 (London: The Hogarth Press, 1955), p. 13.

4 Ibid., pp. 23, 36.

5 *The Standard Edition of the Complete Psychological Works of Sigmund Freud*, trans. and ed. James Strachey, vol. 12 (London: The Hogarth Press, 1964), p. 209.

6 Ibid., p. 210.

7 Ibid., p. 211.

8 "Drunk Ivan Okhlobystin Again Disgraced: Putin's Accomplice Wants to Go to Fight in Ukraine," Global Happenings, April 21, 2022, https://globalhappenings.com/entertainment/158090.html, accessed November 4, 2022.

9 Georg Wilhelm Friedrich Hegel, *The Phenomenology of Spirit*, trans. and ed. Terry Pinkard (Cambridge: Cambridge University Press, 2018).

10 Jean Hyppolite, *Genesis and Structure of Hegel's "Phenomenology of Spirit,"* trans. Samuel Cherniak and John Heckman (Evanston, IL: Northwestern University Press, 1974), p. 37.

11 Alexandre Kojève, *Introduction to the Reading of Hegel: Lectures on the "Phenomenology of Spirit,"* ed. Allan Bloom, trans. James H. Nichols Jr. (Ithaca, NY: Cornell University Press, 1980)

12 Hegel, *The Phenomenology of Spirit* (see note 9), p. 276.

13 Ibid., p. 277.

14 Ibid., p. 279.

15 Ibid.

16 Hyppolite, *Genesis and Structure* (see note 10), p. 372.

17 Hegel, *The Phenomenology of Spirit* (see note 9), p. 280.

18 Ibid.

19 Hyppolite, *Genesis and Structure* (see note 10), p. 370.

20 Walter Benjamin, "The Work of Art in the Age of Mechanical Reproduction," in *Illuminations: Essays and Reflections*, ed. Hannah Arendt, trans. Harry Zohn (New York: Schocken, 1969), pp. 216–60, here p. 241.

21 Georges Bataille, "The Psychological Structure of Fascism," trans. Carl R. Lovett, *New German Critique* 16 (1979): pp. 64–87, here p. 86.

22 Ibid., pp. 73, 72, 82.

23 Ibid., pp. 82, 77.

24 Ibid., p. 77.

25 Ibid., pp. 77–78.

26 Georges Bataille, *The Accursed Share: An Essay on General Economy*, vol. 1, *Consumption*, trans. Robert Hurley (New York: Zone Books, 1988), p. 28.

27 Ibid., pp. 29, 33.

28 Ibid., pp. 34–35.

29 Ibid., p. 21.

→ →

This series of photographs by
Wolfgang Rappel was part of the steirischer
herbst '22 group project *Kartografie der Lücke*
(Mapping the Gap, 2022). It addressed the
history of the Styrian town of Wagna as a
former temporary camp for refugees from
World Wars I and II.

→ →

Undead (Excerpt)

Keti Chukhrov

Ochamchira, a small town in the southwest of the former USSR.

Characters

LEMA. *(Acronym for Lenin, Engels, Marx), a former teacher of history at the town school. After the siege, in the absence of other teachers, she taught mathematics and music.*

KLAVA. *Ex-bookkeeper at the bread factory, ill with poliomyelitis from birth.*

SVETIK. *Brother to Lema and her slave at the moment.*

BATAL. *Drug addict and another brother to Lema.*

TONCHIK. *Ex-militia man, Lema's fiancé.*

ILONA. *The artist, Lema's niece, formerly lived in the same town, but managed to escape with refugee status to the Netherlands to study. She has now returned to the town to make a film reportage.*

PLATON. *A noncharacter who thought he was a character, but was mistaken, because he is dead. One of the founders of the communist party in the region, father of Lema, Batal, and Svetik.*

LEMA: Tonchik, are you ready for a genuine life?
Are you ready for zeal?

TONCHIK: I am very much ready for it.

BATAL: Maybe we should bury Svetik in the sea,
Let's throw him into the water,
Your wedding will be in the water then.

LEMA: This then would be a baptism,
We need a way out from the situation thus created,
But to find this way out, we need to comprehend
        what the situation was about.

KLAVA: It is not enough—merely life and death,
Merely world, merely people,
Merely your own self and all else, merely universe.
The Greeks arranged tragic actions precisely
        because death did not suffice,
Even the most ineffable mercy was scarce,
And unforgettable love or inconsolable grief—were
        insufficient too.
That's why they had to play,
Since one can only play that it's a pity to die or to
        lose,
One can only play there is pain,
And that the war moves you and is worth
        mentioning.
Although no one cared any more, everything was
        somehow, or in fact no-how . . .
That's when they took fear,
No, not even that, they were just not afraid
        anymore,
They were neither dead nor alive by then,
—Nothing would help,
What remained was only a play.

BATAL: Why would you, Klava, need to play
        someone,
You only have a couple of hours left on this Earth.

KLAVA: You're repeating yourself, babe.
I decided who I will be as long as I'm alive,
I will be Glenn Gould.

ILONA: You don't play the piano.

KLAVA: But I studied the soul of Glenn.
The sufferings of our hearts are so much alike.
Yes, I am not able to play the piano,
Now I will perform *The Art of Fugue* for you,
I will thereby tell you what happens in a fugue.

BATAL: Why don't we silence this bullshitting
    corpse?

KLAVA: Well, the first counterpoint begins with the
    cautious introduction of a theme,
The voices then grow so inquisitive,
As if inquiring:
How to get it done so that
Everything that is not yours were as precious as
    something that belongs to you,
And what is your own, but alien to all else,
Could be loved by everyone as something most
    dear.

LEMA: You stupid, it's all otherwise in *The Art of
    Fugue*:
There are two roads in there,
Whoever runs with them, reaches the victory:
One road is short, the other is long,
The two most devoted friends are running along
    them,
Neither knows which road is shorter,
And while they run, their friendship wanes.

Translated from the Russian by Anastasia Osipova

Magda Toffler or An Essay on Silence
(Excerpt)

Boris Nikitin

Part Two

They say it takes 600 repetitions for a new synapse
        to form in the human brain.
In science, this is called plasticity.

Magda is an eloquent person. She speaks six
        languages. She likes to talk. About others, but
        also often about herself.

There is only one thing she doesn't talk about:
        the war and the time immediately afterward.
Never.
She says she can't.

Her father, Paul Toffler, a Catholic pharmacist
        from Trenčin who ran two pharmacies in this
        small town in Western Slovakia, was caught by
        the SS in 1944 when he was secretly supplying
        the partisans with medication.
He was arrested, taken away to Buchenwald, and
        died on a death march shortly before the end
        of the war.

"He died in the concentration camp because he
        gave medicine to the partisans."
That is the only sentence I will ever hear from
        Magda about that time.
She doesn't want to talk about it.
It depresses her, she says.

Those are the last years in which this country is still
        called Czechoslovakia.
We visit my grandparents twice a year, once
        in summer and once in winter to celebrate
        Christmas.

The customs check at the border always takes
        several hours.
The car has to be completely emptied. The border
        guards search the suitcases, the trunk, and the
        entire engine under the hood before we are
        finally allowed to cross the border.

My grandparents live in an old flat in a residential
area not far from the station. The flat is a bit
run-down. The kitchen, the bathroom, and
the toilet are much older than back home in
Switzerland.

There's always a peculiar smell in the rooms that
I only know from this flat and that is so firmly
imprinted in my memory that even today I can
recall it immediately at any time.
At some point, someone explains to me that the
smell is camphor, but I never found out what
that is or what it looks like.

Outside, on the right side of the apartment
building, a staircase leads to the top of a hill
and to a large, spacious park.
It is a Soviet military cemetery, which we visit
regularly.
There is a great view of the city from up there.
But what fascinates me most are the monumental
statues, their giant faces gazing into the future,
solemnly but also incredibly confidently.

My siblings and I spend most of our time with our
grandfather, Emil.
He is Magda's second husband and our mother's
father.
He's a retired lawyer. At the beginning of the
postwar period, he joined the resistance
against the new regime, we are told.
They gave him two years in prison for that.
He never talks about it.
Later, Magda would always say that he got his
cancer there.

In the summers, we always go to the lake with Emil
to swim and fish.

He is a very loving and gentle grandfather, almost
like from a children's book.

We eat ice cream from the ice cream machine and
    collect grasses, which we put in a book between
    sheets of blotting paper and leave there to dry
    for a period of several weeks.
Every now and then we visit Magda at her
    workplace.
It is a pharmaceutical laboratory. The people who
    work there wear white coats, hold ampoules in
    their hands, and take notes.
There is an energy of concentration and busyness.
    Magda runs the lab and everyone calls her
    Professor.

In the evenings we always sit in the living room
    and watch *Zeit im Bild*, the Austrian public
    television news program.

Magda explains to me that the person who has
    been on TV so much recently is the new
    General Secretary of the Communist Party of
    the Soviet Union.
With him, things will get better, she says.
Not much later, I will be standing with her and Emil
    and 10,000 other people at the side of road,
    waving a little flag at this man as he roars past
    us smiling from a black limousine.

Also from the television in the living room, we hear
    the word "Plitvice" on several evenings.
Its syllables are etched into my memory like three
    knife strokes.
It's the name of a park where, apparently, shots
    were fired.
Magda and Emil sit next to me. They have the same
    worried look as the newsreader.
It is the beginning of the Yugoslav Wars, but no one
    knows that at the time.

And there's this photo of Magda's father. Paul
    Toffler.

It is always in the same place on her desk, opposite
    the TV set on the other side of the room,
    showing a person with a high forehead and a
    moustache.
It attracts me every time I visit.
Once I ask Magda whether she thinks he looks a bit
    like Walt Disney.
She turns away from me and walks out of the room
    without giving a reply.

The image of the silent man with the moustache
    looks at me unsuspectingly like a religious
    icon.

"He died in the concentration camp because he
    gave medicine to the partisans."
"He died in the concentration camp because he
    gave medicine to the partisans."

It's a phrase I hear over and over again throughout
    my childhood.
For me, it belongs to the world of my grand-
    parents, just like the sooty houses with their
    bullet-ridden facades, Emil's never-ending
    chemotherapy, or Magda's chronic fatigue. Or
    like the rough, exhausted faces of the people on
    the trams, all of which together form their own
    reality, which we migrate in and out of with our
    parents, and later, after their divorce, with our
    mother, and which we are a part of, but also not,
    when my siblings and I are still children.

And so, twenty years later, it does not surprise me
    that the war and the memory of her father's
    disappearance come back to haunt Magda
    now and begin to mix with her reality in this
    hospital, as I sit with her in the garden of the
    clinic and stroke her skin with my hand.
I spend a week in Bratislava. When I'm not with
    Magda in the clinic, I have lunch with my aunt
    and my two cousins, I visit the castle, walk

along the Danube, take photos, and write
down my thoughts in a notebook.

The city has changed a lot in the past few years.
The facades have been renovated and the city
center has gussied itself up with restaurants
and cafés for tourists and for a new generation.

And I realize:
This is goodbye.

Syargey Prylutsky

170

your daughter was buried behind the house
your father will be forever missing
the house key is lost
photos from peaceful times have burned down
there is nothing to look at
for the reassurance that life here was different once

who is that inside your memories?
the tongue fails to feel their names
whose ashen faces are blurred by time?
who is missing from the new photos?
those who knew
have also been killed

for weeks we made a bed on the floor but didn't sleep
shells became common like birds
we lay down and heard someone's child say:
goodbye
goodbye to everyone
and goodbye to mama
I love you, maybe we will die now
and a heart vibrated along with the vibrating
    building
and plaster fell and fell

Nothing Not to Be Afraid Of

here is a landscape that no longer exists
only the air vibrates between the horizons

a man in the background
and those in the front
they too are no more

we always bought wine here
and here the bakery has reopened
on the right—the bread of the earth
on the left—heavenly bread
which yesterday wasn't given to us

we walk through a former park
on the landmined lawn
we did not even notice
how this sub-spring passed
how unbearable is the reek of this sub-summer

we neither live nor die
in the surviving building
survivors by chance

nothing is surprising anymore
nothing's left not to be afraid of

who is it not calling us
over there behind the shot-through window?
let's greet him farewell

Translated from the Belarusian by Valzhyna Mort

The Rose

there is an island far away
where eerie sprites of darkness play
there is no sky
that hangs above it
no water
round its shores

war is something empty
nauseated soil

bam
bam
bam
there in the wild
a rusty rose blooms, her scent
like clotted blood

in her bud:
yellow snails of heads, red
worms of soldiers
move slowly, moths from the houses
burst into flame
in her bud

she's a riddle of layers, bills
on top of banknotes

her roots, intestines, burble underground
bursting with realm upon realm,
her gut laughs, digesting the district,
her breath is warfare
through leaden nostrils,
her petals—human thigh bones

her roots are lilac throats, there's three,
her kisser a casket, warfare

our failure to act
right now is an action
in itself

were we born to trample roses like her
or to swallow balls of gas?

from under the earth
her image emerges, seen only
by the poor,
and other blooms watch over her:
rambling buttercups of border guards,
zinc bolls
of bluebells

beside them sleeps the gardener, eyes pasted shut,
shrouded in a cassock he bowed to an icon before
     bed
and even in his sleep
in the desire of night and the desire of the rose
he jabs a thorny gunshot wound

beside him stands a wizened boy
he holds a faceless orb
each night
he bows to her, defenseless,
with a face full of holes
his inner shrine is fiery, sheltered
by a blighted burqa
his heart's in kurdistan
but in his heart a broken jaw
travels back and forth

lovers still bear roses
russians in golden chains
in the stench of vapor-vestments
reduced to dust by radium

he leans toward her
maggots in his temples and says,
"remember the ceremonial dawn over the kremlin?

soon,
soon the gardener will wake,
the night will be over …"

she's silent
her legs are covered with the moss of funeral
      wreaths
a diamond gas mask round her solid waist
delirious beetles eat
her womb
her pomegranate breasts tremble
with agitation

soon the gardener will wake

he knows the rose is everywhere but she grows
in the light of weeping galaxies
she wipes tears from the sky and from your face
the septic shawl of the lusterless sun

she frees the unshorn animals within us

for the rose there are no words, no differences
her image exists only
for the voiceless
the victor doesn't turn around
at the sound of a blood-curling cry, he melts
in armored decorations
in a cage he clings to his bird-language
and nourishes the rose
with his old blood
with the body of his mother
with balls of gas

better that your mother is far away in flames
or with a black bag over her head
she walks on the edge of the city
this place where you appeared
trickles with black,
a raving soldier,

bridegroom of the rose of bones,
a small, gifted
precious load
in a robust package
he's torn into as many pieces

as nights
this war will go on
each night she will be your bride
at an abandoned military base your relics will soon
become an explosive wave of youth,
steel beetles
will occupy what was your throat,
they'll buzz:
bam
bam
bam

hot-headed she'll squeeze your eyes and testicles
one by one
she'll slice off your war-
head
your sheets are screen wipes
and they murmur:
bam
bam
bam

she'll screw you with a tiny flame
suck everything dry
to the very last drop, she'll swallow,
you'll be white without
and black within
you'll be white, dead, proved right,
drained of color.

you've died, but you're still
here, again you lie flat and she
chews your head with faded
lips and whispers:
bam
bam
bam

i'll cut you open like a bulb
on the rickety table of ruins

bam
bam
bam
in syria

the syrian rose
bam
bam
bam

her delicate black throat coils:
her complex arsenal
of aromas,
like the web feed you watch before you disappear
without a trace,
she's ablaze with scarlet loss,
what does your terror smell like,
bandages, urine, or gunpowder?

another book,
the book's in her
there's
a bus overturned
on the edge of donbas
like an empty page

this book's been leaking for years,
its reader a literary tick,
that's latched on to skinned pelts of letters
it sucks heat from the spine of the book

do you loathe the book
as much as we
loathe war
unleashed in petals
with ribbons of stock-market tapeworms
with caterpillars of unhinged tyrants
with monumental turn-
coats of knotty barbs

what do you feel, gardener,
when you prune in your sleep

the thorn of syria
the dead leaves of afghanistan
pouring poison
on donbas's rigid stems
cultivating the sour odor
of chechen petals

an exquisite rose,
from her chest emerges
shrapnel
a mutant monster
a bomb, a steel beetle
with scarlet wings
embedded in the body
of the mini-drone-beast
into the thicket
it buzzes

radium

explosive rose

rosa aphasia

rosa contusia

bam
bam
bam
on the dancefloor of war where black techno plays
we all dance
we all concur

an exquisite war-rose
her projection

her noise breaks the bones of the dancing
with steel beats
her noise stitches up eyes
and places a one-hryvnia coin
on the eyelids
with a hollow show of grief

black black techno
for beautiful white bodies
and a disco-
ball the shade of khaki
and shades of khaki
they dance in liquid filth

the simmering bog of the dancefloor
blind beer
spurts from the throat
like a fountain

Translated from the Russian by Helena Kernan

Dana Kavelina

It was in agony that he was resurrected. He delivered himself anew from the grave, it hurt, it took
a while for his memory to return, sagging muscles,
just opened his eyes and the feast was already
underway, look at those sweet bunny rabbits, and
he was just about to bleed out, his back all covered
in cuts, his hands aching, but they led him straight
to the table for the feast, and poured him a drink.

You will have to get in line for resurrection. You
can sign up on the phone, they will call you back,
the wait is long. The resurrected require clothes,
food, housing, and documents. Bureaucracy. There
aren't enough powdered eggs for everyone, and
you cannot heat the entire world.

More humanitarian aid for Easter is on its way
from Europe.
They showed new Kinder Surprises for Ukraine
on TV. A small coffin comes out of the egg. There
is a piggy or a dog inside, and inside that, there is
a cloud or a clock face, and it ticks like a siren if
you put it to your ear. Easter edition 2022.

They fairly divided one egg into fifteen pieces.
Two of them took their bits to the dead in the yard.

A dead dog suddenly rose up on Easter.

Russian soldiers carry baby chicks in their ball
sacks, but these chicks will never hatch. They
would love to give them away, but they can't.
They don't have the proper orders. They weep.

The chicken keeps running without yet quite
noticing that its head has been cut off.
It runs ahead, machine gun at the ready.

The flour for the Easter *kulich* is from ground
bones.

It's there everybody will meet, at the festive table.

Their relatives were snatched from the feast like teeth pulled out by an evil doctor from the gums. Mama's tooth, mother-in-law's tooth, great-uncle's drunken tooth, all stolen and ground into flour. They delivered some little Ukrainian Easter *paska* to the Pope, and he choked on the nails.

Jesus Christ, wait for the others, don't leave us behind.

The ruins of Easter bread. A sprinkling of old photographs, some other life out there, a long time ago. White eggshell ruins.

Feed me, please. With various cloud-shaped debris, dust porridge. Possibly even siren soup. We'll drink your drool then, melt the snow, make tea. Everything is delicious at the campfire, artisan-smoked.

In the wintertime, we still had tea. Now we stoke the fire with apple blossom, which quickly turns to cinders.

They began to distinguish one another's faces in the dark. They began to see with their backsides whenever they surfaced. They would bring porridge to the dead, too, and greet the drones with various secret signals.

On the egg, he draws wreaths and crosses as well as names. And also the faces of everyone in the basement, he carefully signed them: those who devoured time. On the dial, meanwhile, a coun-tenance appeared. An egg countenance. The dog offered itself for dinner. They declined and invited it to the table. The table was empty. The tablecloth shone like the sun against the ruins, all in snow. "He has risen," the dog guessed. He's on his way.

They prepared paints from the ashes. Instead of
eggs, they painted each other's faces and hands,
hugging each other all black, like in the Congo.
They collected scattered flour, but not enough,
they have snowball fights, they hug crippled houses.

A rabbit crosses a minefield with a basket for the
children. They would have liked to cook the rabbit
for lunch, but the dead dog is against it. Solidarity
of tired legs.

They took potshots at the eggs again. There were
no yolks inside, only whites. They couldn't decide
whether to be born, and you can't go to war
without feathers. Old hens with machine guns
at the ready, there is no one left to carry the eggs.

Last year's egg ballet is on TV, they've been seduced.

Dazzling white. The egg hatches a plastic tank.

They would have liked to cut up the bread for
everyone. The bread starts screaming. They have to
keep going or the celebration will fall flat. They look
back at the calendar in hope. No, it is today after all.

Just lie in the ground with your eyes closed
for now. We'll be right back.

Once upon a time, beggars were able to sculpt
Easter eggs out of mud, to then spend the night
in their shells.

Now, even the mud is running out for Easter,
you can't find it anywhere.
There is nothing to moisten the dried clods; the
children have drunk up all the spittle.

She cut her hair a month before Easter and buried
it in the ground. Just in case they didn't have enough
hair when they came home the next spring.

Translated from the Russian by David Riff

A *War Vocabulary*

In 1943, while living in Nazi-occupied Warsaw,
Czesław Miłosz, a Polish poet, wrote *The World:
A Naïve Poem*. Most pieces in the collection
serve as explanations of simple words, such as
"Anxiety," "Love," "Hope," "Gate," "Porch," and
"Road"—because war changes the meaning of
words. Some are blunted and need sharpening,
as a knife against a stone. Some become so sharp
you cannot look at them. Some words just die and
fall off. Some emerge from the past and start to be
meaningful again. They gain importance.

I will try to compile such a war vocabulary.
But these will not be poems or any kind of literary
works written by me. All are fragments of mono-
logues, stories of others that I have been listening
to during these grim days. Well, some of them may
be "literarized." Some of them are also translated
from Russian.

People tell their stories at the Lviv railway
station (where waves of internally displaced
persons are rolling in from East to West), at temporary shelters, or in the street, near coffee stands.
Some of them are eager to share, and some of them
are asked gently first, and then they break out like
an unstoppable wave.

I did not record all of the stories myself,
though. Some of them were recorded by co-
authors—Anna Protsuk, Yevhen Klimakin, Oksana
Kurylo, and Dmytro Tkachuk—and some of them
by participants in and witnesses of this war. These
are both their private stories, and stories they have
heard from others.

APPLES, *Anna, Kyiv*
That night I fell asleep in the bathtub, in a bucket
of blankets and pillows, listening to the most
powerful explosions here since the beginning
of the war. Long ago, in a past life, I was crazy in
love, and we went to a house in the Carpathian
Mountains. It was deep in autumn. We fell asleep
in an attic—in a bed that was not much more comfortable than the bathtub—and I listened to apples
hitting the ground everywhere in the garden. The
slamming of the large, ripe apples continued at a
measured pace throughout the night. I was happy.
Now, I fall asleep to the explosions and I hear those
apples. I so badly want it to be those garden apples
hitting the ground around us.

BATH, *Maryna, Kharkiv*
We did not have a shelter close to us, so the
bathroom was our best hope. I never thought that
our whole apartment could shrink to the size of the
bathroom. When the missiles started flying around
us—first, several houses away from ours, and then
just two—I gradually stopped tidying up the apartment and wiping the dust, as though giving up on
it all. It seemed so pointless to me. And then I told
my bathtub, "Let's hope you save me, okay?"
    When a missile hit our yard, I was in the
bathtub. Every single window was blown out,
together with the frames. The kitchen, the
bedroom—the whole floor was covered in glass.
I could never have survived anywhere else. Only
in the bathroom. And guess what? Hot water came
in the next day. I don't know why, but it felt like
an award for something. No lights, but hot water
pouring from the tap! I filled the bathtub with
it and lit some candles. I found some aromatic
oil somewhere. I felt like the character in *One
Thousand and One Nights*, like Scheherazade.
Only I don't count nights anymore.

BEAR, *Anonymous*
My sleep is more real than my day. During the day,
I chase those thoughts in my head away by daily
errands. But in my sleep, reality strikes back. *The
Sleep of Reason Produces Monsters*, Goya said. One
of many meanings of such words now is that you've
got to make yourself think against reality. Today, I
wanted to go back to my childhood. So I "escaped"
to where there is no war. To Makiyivka, to Ust-
Kamenogorsk, to the Zakarpattya of my childhood. The first time, I remembered growing up as
a preschool kid step by step. And now I remember
the bear. Both my own bear, and another one—an
imagined one. Two teddy bears. And either I am
hugging his little self or he, enormous and white
in spots, is hugging me. I am fantasizing, and there
is no war. Let me say it aloud: "fantasy." This word
does sound wonderful, "fantasy."

BEAUTY, *Kateryna*, *Vyshhorod*
I read a story about World War II not so long ago.
There was this girl who wore her mom's worst
clothes to pass by the Nazis unnoticed, to avoid
being raped. I pause near my wardrobe; is it time to
wear the worst already, or can I still make it? Things
change so quickly. The cabs are not coming. Either
the line is busy or they refuse. I will just walk to Kyiv.
    In a time of war, beauty becomes dangerous.
Beautiful things, people, relationships—
nowadays they don't exist to inspire. They exist
to be annihilated. Not for admiration and loving
touches, but for pain.
    My boots get stuck in the mud along the
highway. My phone beeps with an SMS: "You
have just visited our beauty parlor for a manicure.
Please, leave a review."

BULLET, *Mykola*, *Khmelnytskyi*
I don't know if I took a sin upon my soul. I just aim,
and I fire, but I close my eyes while firing. Whether
my bullet kills someone or not, one can only guess.

CANARY, *Olya*, *Irpin*

When we were fleeing Irpin, there was this moment
when it went so quiet. A house stood nearby that
was hit by missiles. All the windows were broken,
the entrance was blocked. And it was at that
moment that I heard a canary through one of the
windows. I used to have a canary when I was a kid,
so I always recognize that sound. It must have gone
down to a bomb shelter and did not have a chance
to come back up. So much happened before and
after that, but I cannot forget that canary.

CAVE, *Roman*, *Chernihiv*

My whole life, I was into speleology. When I had
a free weekend, I would pack my gear and go
exploring caves. There is a large bomb shelter in
our neighborhood, under a school. For the first
couple of days, there was no light there. I came in
wearing a headlamp; it was quiet inside. It seemed
that there was no one there. And suddenly, I saw
people. I saw children crammed in by the walls. All
those people were like stalagmites and stalactites.
It seemed as though they had been there for thousands of years. That's what war does to time.

COCOA, *Bohdana*, *Lviv*

Yesterday there were a lot of people from
Kramatorsk, a whole bunch of them. The trains kept
coming, and so would the people, for some food
and conversation. At the time, we were serving rice
porridge with milk, a typical morning meal, and
one I didn't like. We were running out of coffee, and
we thought we'd start making cocoa. Grown-ups
like drinking cocoa—they are just too ashamed to
acknowledge it. I was looking for green tea among
the packs of black. I made jokes that we could feed
half of Ukraine with Polish tuna because our storage
room was so full of it. In it, we found half-liter water
bottles, and digging through lots of cans of pâté,
I found a full box of chocolate candies for the kids.
They had striped green wrapping, like tiny watermel-
ons. Daily chores, small joys, tuna, the usual stuff.

But today they hit the Kramatorsk railway
station. And there is this thought I cannot get out
of my head—that over thirty people won't drink
any more coffee, won't ask for tea, won't give their
children candies in the striped wrapping. I won't be
able to get them to eat a tuna sandwich. They were
headed to us. We had already found coffee for them.
 I don't know if there is anything beyond this
world. But if there is, they should have the tastiest
cocoa there.

DWELLINGS, *Dmytro*, *Kyiv*
Observing the houses, we saw smashed kitchens,
remnants of bedrooms, wallpapers from children's
rooms, pieces of mirrors from bathrooms. As
we looked at them, we realized that some of the
owners of these apartments had been saving
money for half of their lives to build and fill these
dwellings. Some of them were probably planning
to spend their whole lives there.
 We saw a billboard in front of one of the
buildings that read, "At last, some affordable space
for you."

FOOD, *Oksana*, *Lviv*
I got to host a family from the East for a night.
I showed them to the kitchen and said, "There is
the kitchen, you can take the food on the table."
 At these words, they started crying.
 "You can take the food on the table."

FREEDOM, *Vadym*, *Konotop*
Freedom is such a thing—nobody is going to get
it for you. Nobody will give you freedom, you won't
get it as a present for yourself, you can't wait for
it to arrive. You only get to make it for yourself. Yes,
handmade. There are no freedom factories. It's not
batch production.

GRANNIES, *Yuri*, *Kharkiv*
The apartments of two grannies from the opposite
building were ruined, and they did not want to

go to someone else's apartment, because it was
someone else's. So they were just sitting on a bench
near the entrance like that. And there they died
from shrapnel. And there we buried them, in the
yard, digging holes between the shelling.

LETTERS, *Nina*, *Konotop*
I've been thinking about memory a lot. We never
really know what our mind is capable of.

My husband was a geologist, he traveled all
over the Soviet Union. Sometimes he would spend
several months beyond the Arctic Circle and write
me letters from there. There were postcards of a
special kind—he would send me those instead of
the typical ones. I received forty-three in total. And
so, when packing for the bomb shelter, I put them
all in the bag. Some people took books, and I took
those letters. *I'll be reading those in there*, I thought.
But I couldn't really, the light was very poor, so I
would just pick each one up and remember what
was written. I haven't read them for ages, but they
lived somewhere in my memory.

Then, when I went through all the letters,
I started coming up with answers in my mind.
Because, I am ashamed to say, I did not write
him back often. And when I did, I was quite brief.
Now I started coming up with long and eloquent
replies. But I did not mention the war to him, nor
the shelter. Why would he need to know? I only
told him that the winter turned out quite long this
time around.

LIFE, *Violetta*, *Mariupol*
International Women's Day, March 8, is my favorite
holiday. But this spring in Mariupol, I expected
neither presents nor flowers. My sister and I took
some plastic bottles and went looking for water.
Something started roaring around the neighborhood, but we initially thought it was on the
opposite side. And then I heard a whistling sound
coming toward us, and I told my sister to squat.
I did not want to fall down, as the ground was

wet. My sister stood there as if frozen. Maybe she couldn't believe it, maybe she was afraid to seem awkward. An explosion erupted, then soil flew up and started falling down on us. We started running. And when we looked back, we saw someone sitting on a bench near the entrance to the building, right next to where the explosion occurred. Wrapped in a pink blanket, she must have been enjoying the sun outdoors. We saw her lean over the bench and fall down unnaturally.

On this March 8, life and death were rationed out to us women. We got life.

PRAGUE, A *Teenage Girl*, *Kharkiv*
I am that person who always puts everything off. I would even put off having a tasty treat when I was a kid so that I could eat it later in a nice setting with candles, or [while] watching a cool movie. And then you taste them, and they're not tasty anymore. That's how I always wanted to experience Prague, like a postponed treat. We have relatives there. But I hadn't had the time to go. And now, finally, I am going there, but there is no happiness.

SHOWER, *Oleksandr*, *Bucha*
I don't recommend taking a shower while under heavy shelling. You lose the enjoyment of the whole process. There is this annoying thought in your mind: *If I get hit by shells anytime now, I'll become a victim of war with a soapy bare butt.*

SILENCE, *Ulyana*, *Lviv*
The puppet theater became a shelter for the displaced. We put mattresses on its stages, in its halls, in its foyer. In the beginning, there were a lot of people with children and animals. For two days straight, they were lying silently on those mattresses. I have never seen so many silent people and animals in one place. Then, they livened up a little. But I will never forget that silence. It was scary.

STAR, *Romanna*, *Kyiv*
When the windows are taped to prevent glass
from shattering during explosions, they are like
stars. I did it with my windows, too. Opaque tape,
four stripes crosswise on every window, just like
the manual says. Whenever the sun is out, you can
see shadows from the tape on the walls. Like stars
moving slowly.
 I would like this to be my only memory of
the war.

STAR, *Victoria*, *Kharkiv*
Once we thought that we did not have any tradi-
tions in our household, so we made a Christmas
star—a huge one, very tall. It was so tall that it had
to be carried like a spear into the apartment in
our five-story building. We screwed in some light
bulbs, as well. Then we learned some carols—only
the Ukrainians have carols, right? Well, that kind
of carol, at least. And so, we went caroling. We
made so much money during the first year that we
even got to sew some long costumes for ourselves.
People started commissioning us. Our relatives,
friends, even strangers.
 That star is still there on my balcony.

SUN, *Nina*, *Konotop*
When the war started, I thought, *I will cry a lot.*
'Cause that's who I am, a crybaby. But here I am
now, plugged up. Not one tear all these days. I
cried only once when, after sitting in a shelter for
a long time, I went outside and saw the sun. And I
burst into tears. I was walking home like that, and
I couldn't understand whether it was a real cry or
just tears dropping.

TETRIS, *Anna*, *Kyiv*
A dark, dark train, full of bright hopes. Dimmed
screens, everyone reading the news. From time to
time they talk in a whisper, tuck their children in,
and pet some strangers' cats.
 Everyone is family.

When we were kids, we played *Tetris* just to be
able to place nine people and three animals in one
car compartment.

TICKETS, *Olya*, *Lviv*
I keep thinking there is a parallel life somewhere.
Where we are as we were before the war.
There is this family zoo near Kyiv. They
are asking people to buy tickets even though
everything is burned down, just so they can afford
to feed the animals that survived. I bought a few
yesterday, and I imagined us strolling through
it with our friends, feeding the lambs from our
hands, taking pictures with the ostriches. [And we
were] so happy.
It was like a picture from those religious
brochures about heaven on earth. Do you think
we will ever use those tickets?

TRASH, *Kateryna*, *Vyshhorod*
February 24. Russian helicopters were passing our
windows, missiles were hitting the ground. *I have
to leave. I have to take the trash out.* I took the bag
with organic waste. *Should I take the bag with the
plastic, with the glass, with the paper? Will it all end
up mixed together in the chaos of war? The carefully
washed yogurt jars, the bottles, the children's coloring
books* …
Will my house, my city, become trash once
I leave it?
Am I even entitled to think about it?

WAREHOUSE, *Kateryna*, *Vyshhorod*
I watered my flowers and left. They have been
without water for over a month now. When the
Russians retreated from my city, my mother
wanted to take care of the flowers. She was ready
to spend three hours on the road to get there.
People were waiting for a commuter train,
and there was a freight train standing on the next
track. They were unloading something from it
to a warehouse hangar. That warehouse was well

known to me; we used to exchange wastepaper for books there when we were kids.

All of a sudden, my mother felt dizzy; her feet became unsteady, she barely made it back home. For the rest of the day, she felt nauseous.

The warehouse that once contained books became the warehouse of human bodies.

WEDDING, *Violetta*, *Mariupol*
We celebrated my brother's wedding on February 22. We were so happy that rumors about the war had not played out. But then, a week or a week and a half later, my brother and his wife had to flee Mariupol. They packed a suitcase and took it to the highway to exit the city. I wrote "Zaporizhzhya" on a piece of cardboard for them, so that they could try to catch a car there. That's how they set out on their "honeymoon," on the first trip of their marriage.

Translated from the Ukrainian by Taras Malkovych

Editors' Biographies

EKATERINA DEGOT is an art historian, researcher, and curator focusing on aesthetic and sociopolitical issues in Russia and Eastern Europe from the 19th century to the post-Soviet era. She began her tenure as director and chief curator of steirischer herbst in 2018. From 2014 to 2017, Degot was artistic director of the Academy of the Arts of the World in Cologne. Among other shows, she curated the First Ural Industrial Biennial in Yekaterinburg (2010, with Cosmin Costinas and David Riff) and headed the first Bergen Assembly with David Riff (2013).

DAVID RIFF is a writer, translator, artist, curator, and former member of the art group Chto Delat. He has been a curator at steirischer herbst since 2018. Among other shows, Riff cocurated the First Ural Industrial Biennial in Yekaterinburg (2010, with Cosmin Costinas and Ekaterina Degot) and headed the first Bergen Assembly together with Ekaterina Degot (2013). His most recent effort as an artist-curator was a large-scale exhibition on Mikhail Lifshitz in Moscow (2018, with Dmitry Gutov).

Contributors' Biographies

KETI CHUKHROV is an art theorist, philosopher, playwright, and poet. Her latest book *Practicing the Good: Desire and Boredom in Soviet Socialism* (2020) deals with the impact of socialist political economy on the epistemes of historical socialism. Chukhrov's work as a playwright incorporates poetry, drama, performance, music, and video. Her films *Love-machines* (2013) and *Communion* (2016) made after her dramatic poems were featured at the Bergen Assembly (2013), *Specters of Communism* (James Gallery, New York, 2015), and the Ljubljana Triennial U3 (2016). Her play *Global Congress of Post-Prostitution* premiered at steirischer herbst '19.

MAJA HADERLAP writes poetry, prose, and essays in Slovenian and German and translates from Slovenian into German. She won the 2011 Ingeborg Bachmann Prize with the novel *Engel des Vergessens*—translated into English as *Angel of Oblivion* (2016)—and also published the poetry collection *langer transit* (2014) and *Im langen Atem der Geschichte* (2018). Haderlap has received numerous prizes and awards, most recently the Max Frisch Prize of the City of Zurich (2018), the Austrian Art Prize for Literature (2019), and the Christine Lavant Prize (2021).

DANA KAVELINA lived in Kyiv and Lviv before fleeing to Germany. She is a graduate of the Department of Graphic Arts at the National Technical University of Ukraine and works mainly with animation and video, but also with installation, painting, and graphics. Her works often address military violence and war from a gender perspective. They are particularly concerned with the position of the victim as a political subject, as well as the distance between historical and individual trauma. Kavelina's works are almost universally based on her own poetry and prose texts, which she weaves into complex visual-linguistic forms.

OLEXII KUCHANSKYI is an independent researcher, film curator, and writer whose main interests lie in experimental moving-image art, collective visual practices, their ecological impact, and critical cultures of nature. S/he was born in Vinnytsia, Ukraine, and lives in Kyiv and Lviv, Ukraine. His/her works have been published in *Prostory*, *Your Art*, *TransitoryWhite*, *Political Critique*, *East European Film Bulletin*, *Arts of the Working Class*, *Moscow Art Magazine*, *e-flux Notes*, *Theory on Demand*, and others. S/he was a member of Occupy Kyiv Cinemas, an activist network protecting Kyivan communal property cinemas at risk of privatization.

MICHAEL MARDER is Ikerbasque Research Professor in the Department of Philosophy at the University of the Basque Country (UPV/EHU), Vitoria-Gasteiz. His writings span the fields of ecological theory, phenomenology, and political thought. He is the author of numerous scholarly articles and monographs, including *Plant-Thinking* (2013), *Phenomena—Critique—Logos* (2014), *The Philosopher's Plant* (2014), *Dust* (2016), *Energy Dreams* (2017), *Heidegger* (2018), *Political Categories* (2019), *Pyropolitics* (2015, 2020), *Dump Philosophy* (2020), *Hegel's Energy* (2021), *Green Mass* (2021), and *Philosophy for Passengers* (2022).

BORIS NIKITIN is a theater director and author, considered one of the most important voices in contemporary German-language theater. Since 2007, his productions, texts, and happenings have dealt with the representation of identity and reality, blurring the boundary between illusionist theater and performance, between documentary and propaganda. In 2017, Nikitin was awarded the City of Jena's Jakob Michael Reinhold Lenz Prize for his complete works. In 2020, he received the Swiss Theater Prize. His piece *Erste Staffel: 20 Jahre Big Brother* was invited to the Mülheimer Theatertage in 2021 as one of the best German-language plays.

MARTIN POLLACK is a journalist, writer, and literary translator. Between 1987 and 1998, he was an editor at *Der Spiegel*, with stints as a foreign correspondent in Vienna and Warsaw. At the same time, Pollack published essays and translations of Polish literature. Since 1998, he has been a freelance author and translator. Pollack's books aim to document events accurately without imposing personal views on the reader. They mostly deal with forgotten events from recent history, including 20th-century crimes in Galicia. His latest books include *Der Kaiser von Amerika: Die große Flucht aus Galizien* (2010), *Kontaminierte Landschaften* (2014), *Topografie der Erinnerung* (2016), and *Die Frau ohne Grab: Bericht über meine Tante* (2019).

SYARGEY PRYLUTSKY has participated in numerous literary festivals and slam competitions. He is the author of five volumes of poetry, including his debut collection *Dzievianostyja forever* (2008). His most recent publication is the Belarusian-Ukrainian book *Eurydyka ne azyraetstsa / Evrydyka ne ohliadyvaetsia* (2020). Under the pseudonym Sirożka Pistonczyk, he published the short prose volumes *Jopyty dvuch maladych nieliudziau*

(together with Vlasik Smarkach) and *Dehienieratyuny slounik*. He was a three-time finalist in the Belarusian PEN Center's Young Writers Competition. Prylutsky translates from Ukrainian, Polish, and English. He lives in Bucha, Kyiv Oblast.

GALINA RYMBU is a poet, critic, curator of literary projects, and queer feminist of Moldovan-Ukrainian origin. Since 2018 she has been living in Lviv, where she cofounded the nomadic Institute of Land States with poet Janis Sinaiko. She is the author of two poetry collections, and her poems have been translated into numerous languages. The English translation of her debut, *Life in Space* (2020), was shortlisted for the Derek Walcott Prize. Rymbu is also the founder and editor of *F-Pis' mo*, a journal of feminist and LGBTIQ+ literature and theory, as well as the contemporary poetry website *Gryoza*. She also founded and curated the Arkady Dragomoshchenko Poetry Prize (2014–21).

MARCIA SÁ CAVALCANTE SCHUBACK is a professor of philosophy at Södertörn University. The translator of Heidegger's *Being and Time* into Portuguese, she specializes in German idealism, hermeneutical phenomenology, and contemporary philosophy. Her books include *The Beginning of God: An Inquiry into Schelling's Late Philosophy* (1998) and *Praise of Nothingness: Essays on Philosophical Hermeneutics* (2006).

OSTAP SLYVYNSKY is a poet, translator, essayist, and literary scholar, author of five volumes of poetry in Ukrainian and seven books of poetry in translation. Slyvynsky translates fiction and scholarly literature from English, Belarusian, Bulgarian, Macedonian, and Polish and has received numerous literary and translation awards, most recently the Special Prize of the UNESCO City of Literature Lviv

(2020). Slyvynsky is also the curator of Propisi, a workshop festival for young writers. He researches and teaches on the literary history of the 20th and 21st centuries in Central and Eastern Europe and is vice president of the Ukrainian PEN Club.

OXANA TIMOFEEVA is a philosopher, a professor at the European University at St. Petersburg, and a leading researcher at Tyumen State University. She is also a member of the artistic collective Chto Delat as well as deputy editor of the journal *Stasis*. Her publications include *Introduction to the Erotic Philosophy of Georges Bataille* (2009), *History of Animals* (2018), *How to Love a Homeland* (2020), and *Solar Politics* (2022).

Matthias Ulbl
Accounting

Kathrin Lazarus
Coordinator Human Resources &
Assistant Archive

Simon Resch
Office Assistant

Danica Radat
Facility Manager

Grupa Ee
(Mina Fina, Damjan Ilić,
Ivian Kan Mujezinović)
Graphic Design

Systemantics
Website

Festival Support

Administration
Anja Herman
Patricia Temmel

Communication
Janosch Böhm
Shirin Hooshmandi
Lilly Jagl
Felicitas Pilz
Luca Rädler
Laura Riedl
Anja Winkler

Visitor Service
Paulina Maitz
Birgit Polzer
Philipp Strohmeier
Elke Tomašič
Paul Wolff

herbst Education
Fides Brogyányi
Paul Gerstl
Laurenz Henkel
Sarah Hollweger

Production Coordinators
Miriam Bacher
A. Tolga Balci
Anna Gynes
Lukas Kaiser
Heinz Leitner
Maria-Oscara Ohrenstein
Martin Pelzmann
Ronny Priesching
Eva Schmartschan
Guggi Schneider
Andreas Schögler
Lisa Schöttel

Festival Drivers
Michael Eisl
Christian Jalen
Marc Leitgeb
Maurice Randa
Johannes Rips
Michael Sladek

Colophon

This book is published in conjunction with steirischer herbst festival steirischer herbst '22—*A War in the Distance*, September 22–October 16, 2022, Graz, Styria, Austria.

This edition of steirischer herbst was curated by Ekaterina Degot, Mirela Baciak, Dominik Müller, Christoph Platz, David Riff, Barbara Seyerl, and Gábor Thury and created by the whole team of steirischer herbst. With curatorial advice by Goran Injac.

Editors:
Ekaterina Degot
David Riff

With contributions by:
Keti Chukhrov, Maja Haderlap, Dana Kavelina, Olexii Kuchanskyi, Michael Marder, Boris Nikitin, Martin Pollack, Syargey Prylutsky, Galina Rymbu, Marcia Sá Cavalcante Schuback, Ostap Slyvynsky, Oxana Timofeeva

Project management:
Fabian Reichel, Hatje Cantz

Managing editor:
Jeff Thoss

Proofreading:
Aaron Bogart

Graphic design:
Grupa Ee (Mina Fina, Damjan Ilić, Ivian Kan Mujezinović)

Production:
Thomas Lemaître, Hatje Cantz

Printing:
Livonia Print Ltd., Riga

Paper:
Munken Print White 1.5, 90 g/m²

© 2023 Hatje Cantz Verlag, Berlin, steirischer herbst, Graz, and authors

© 2022 uniT, Rappel for *Kartografie der Lücke* by Wolfgang Rappel

"The Rose" by Galina Rymbu was first published in *Modern Poetry in Translation*, no. 2, 2020. Reprinted by permission.

"A War Vocabulary" by Ostap Slyvynsky was first published in *Document Journal*, June 2022. Reprinted by permission.

steirischer herbst festival gmbh
Sackstraße 17
8010 Graz, Austria
www.steirischerherbst.at

Published by
Hatje Cantz Verlag GmbH
Mommsenstraße 27
10629 Berlin
www.hatjecantz.com
A Ganske Publishing Group Company

ISBN 978-3-7757-5497-2

Cover illustration:
Grupa Ee

Every effort has been made to trace the copyright holders and obtain permission to reproduce material. Please do get in touch with any enquiries or any information relating to unintended omissions.